offbeat MARIJUANA

The life & times of the world's grooviest plant

by Saul Rubin

Foreword by
Allen F. St. Pierre
Executive Director,
NORML Foundation

with photos by Bill Bridges

SANTA
MONICA
PRESS

All books published by Santa Monica Press LLC are available at special quantity discounts when purchased in bulk by corporations, organizations, or groups. Please call our special sales department at 1-800-784-9553.

Published by:
SANTA MONICA PRESS, LLC
P.O. Box 1076
Santa Monica, CA 90406-1076
1-800-784-9553
www.santamonicapress.com

Printed in the United States

Book and cover design by Susan Landesmann, Susan Landesmann Design.

Rubin, Saul. 1957-
    Offbeat Marijuana : the life & times of the world's grooviest
plant / by Saul Rubin; with photos by Bill Bridges.
        p.   cm.
    Includes bibliographical references.
    ISBN 1-891661-05-1 (pbk.)
    1. Marijuana- -Social aspects. 2. Marijuana- -folklore.
3. Marijuana in popular culture.   I. Title.
GR790.M35R83   1999
398 ' . 368345- -dc21   99-13285
                                              CIP

10 9 8 7 6 5 4 3 2 1

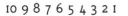

SANTA

MONICA

PRESS

table of contents

Foreword **V**

I. The History of Marijuana **7**
What a Long, Strange Trip It's Been

II. Marijuana and Society **27**
"Book 'Em, Dano"

III. Marijuana in the Workplace **63**
"May I Have Another Cup, Please?"

IV. Marijuana as Medicine **85**
"Smoke Two Joints and Call Me in the Morning"

V. The Marijuana Lab Report **III**
Stoned in the Name of Science

VI. Hemp **131**
The Soybean of the 21st Century

VII. Marijuana in Popular Culture **159**
Reefer Madness

VIII. Pot Culture **199**
"Don't Bogart That Joint, My Friend"

Resources **235**

Permissions **238**

foreword

There is no doubt that the cannabis plant (a.k.a. "marijuana") is the most politicized plant in human history. Bar none.

Yet despite the U.S. government's 62-year blanket prohibition on the myriad uses of cannabis, many of which are well documented in *Offbeat Marijuana*, cannabis remains a popularly consumed intoxicant—second only to alcohol.

Arguably, cannabis is currently the United States' fourth most valuable cash crop with an estimated annual value in excess of $15 billion. In the last statistical year, 1997, state and federal law enforcement agencies arrested more Americans than ever before on cannabis charges—a resource draining 695,000 arrests (87% for possessing small, usable amounts). This translates into an arrest every 45 seconds!

A recent U.S. Department of Justice report indicates that over forty thousand citizens are currently in state and federal prisons solely on cannabis charges.

The U.S. government spends approximately $10 to $12 billion of taxpayer money annually trying to enforce the failed prohibition. Since the early 1970s, the government has been nurturing a massive and pervasive "drug war-prison-industrial complex."

In his award-winning series on cannabis prohibition, published in 1994 by *The Atlantic Monthly*, writer Eric Schlosser begs an important, though rarely asked, question: How does a society go from nearly decriminalizing cannabis for adults in the 1970s to today, where adults are typically punished more severely for growing under 50 cannabis plants for their own personal consumption than long-held, traditional, violent predatory crimes, such as second- and third-degree murder, manslaughter, rape, arson, assault and battery, robbery, and kidnapping?

Offbeat Marijuana offers the reader numerous examples of how such a Kafkaesque premise came true. Whether it's the government-sanctioned *Reefer Madness* scare of the 1930s, the current $2 billion Partnership for a Drug-Free America propaganda campaign, the hundreds of millions of tax dollars that annually pour into the coffers of the DARE program, or the government agencies whose only mission is surviving at the nipple of cannabis prohibition, one thing should be clear: Cannabis prohibition is one of the greatest frauds perpetrated by the U.S. government on citizenry.

Any fair reading of the history of cannabis in the United States cannot conclude otherwise.

The cannabis plant is one of the most versatile and important plants humans have ever interfaced with, be it for non-medical, medical, or industrial use. Indeed, it can be said, despite decades

of heavy-lauded, misguided government efforts to demonize cannabis and the individuals who employ it, cannabis, in every sense of the word, is here for good. Renowned world-traveling ethnobiologist Dr. Richard Evan Shultes says it best, "There can be no doubt that a plant that has been in partnership with man since the beginnings of agricultural efforts, that has served man in so many ways, and that, under the searchlight of modern chemical study, has yielded many new and interesting compounds will continue to be a part of man's economy. It would be a luxury that we could ill afford if we allowed prejudices, resulting from the abuse of cannabis, to deter scientists from learning as much as possible about this ancient and mysterious plant."

—**Allen F. St. Pierre**
Executive Director
NORML Foundation
Washington, D.C.
February 11, 1999

history

what a long, strange trip it's been

the marijuana plant is truly a weed success story. Like an herbal Zelig, marijuana has played a versatile, high-profile role through five thousand stormy years of cultivation. The plant has such great survival instincts that it can change sex as needed and adapts quickly to new climates. It also has a quirky reproductive method. Nearing the end of its spring-to-fall cycle, it relies on a breeze to carry pollen from male stamens to waiting female flowers. This capricious union creates seeds that spill to the ground, germinating next season's crop. In a kind of horticultural shrug, each new generation of the plant literally moves in whatever direction the wind is blowing. Amid the fierce survival battles so common in the wild, along comes a plant that says, "Whatever."

Amid the fierce survival battles so common in the wild, along comes a plant that says, "Whatever."

In its most sobering incarnation, the marijuana plant's hollow stalk has been used for centuries to make vital fiber products, including clothing, rope, and paper. Europeans and early Americans knew it as hemp and considered it a crucial crop. American farmers stopped growing it after the Civil War when demand dropped, but the hemp plant kept right on going. Even today wild hemp continues to crop up across America in areas as diverse as rural pastures and city sewers.

More than just a useful fiber, marijuana has been harvested as a medicine for thousands of years. Various cultures have added it to medicinal teas, extracts, and potions to treat a variety of illnesses, from bronchitis to "absent-mindedness." Chinese medical records show that it was used as far back as five thousand years ago

7

to battle malaria, gout, and to ease the discomfort of menstrual cramps. In the West, marijuana was prescribed for everything from pain relief to convulsions. It was suggested to Queen Victoria by her court physician—with no great fuss—to treat her cramps.

If the marijuana plant's story ended here, it would make for a worthy tale. But it would be one of simple benevolence, lacking complexity and depth. The story doesn't end there, of course—it continues on, further up the stalk, where the plant's darker side enters the picture.

Marijuana survives in blazingly hot regions by secreting a leaf-coating resin that protects it from the sun's dehydrating effects. This heat-shielding nectar is saturated with a compound scientists call tetrahydrocannabinol, commonly referred to as THC. Marijuana contains 400 chemicals and 60 cannabinoids—compounds unique to the plant—but THC is by far the plant's most famous and profound substance. THC has made all the difference for marijuana, infusing its flowering tops and leaves with mind-altering powers. In concentrated form, the intoxicating resin is called hash.

In the West, marijuana was prescribed for everything from pain relief to convulsions. It was suggested to Queen Victoria by her court physician —with no great fuss— to treat her cramps.

Marijuana's most famous substance.

8

An 18th-century Indian nobleman taking a toke off his waterpipe.

The First Toker?

There's no documentation of when a thrill seeker first used marijuana for fun. No record of a "Pothead X," so to speak. But it's a good bet that pot smoking didn't begin in Europe or North America, where most hemp farmers were unaware that right under their noses was a mighty herbal concoction. Even if they had inhaled, they wouldn't have been awed by the experience. Industrial hemp is bred for its fiber, not its killer buds, so it produces low levels of THC. In any case, Americans and Europeans weren't looking for other stimulants during the eighteenth and early nineteenth centuries. They had already found their recreational drugs of choice — tobacco, alcohol, caffeine, and, ultimately, morphine and opium.

This was not the case, however, in the world's hot zones. In Africa, India, and Arabia, word was out early that this was no ordinary weed. In these regions, the plant's historical role as an intoxicant is rich and colorful. The Greek historian Herodotus observed the Scythians of northern Greece practicing a unique burial ritual during the fifth century involving hemp seeds. They would drop the seeds into a fire and then run wildly through the vapors, howling with joy. In India, drinking a tea made from an extract of the plant's resin has been practiced for centuries. Called *bhang*, this stimulating drink is consumed in holy rituals and at informal social gatherings. In Indian folklore, the hemp plant has been called the "joy giver," "the sky flier," "the heavenly guide," "the poor man's heaven," and "the soother of grief."

Not surprisingly, Indians were one of the first populations studied to evaluate the consequences of hemp consumption. The

The leader of the *haschischin*, Hasan-Ibn-Sabah, was known to have directed his followers to take hash.

horrible murders. Because this group was known as the *haschischin*, the Arab word for hash, it was reported that from this word came the English term for "assassin." The lexicography lesson was intended to illustrate the horrors of hemp use. The commissioners weren't impressed, concluding that the moderate use of hemp as a recreational drug wasn't harmful.

Indian Hemp Drugs Commission was convened in 1893 when British authorities became alarmed by rumors circulating about the dangers of hemp drug use. Their concern stemmed from scandalous reports suggesting that hemp drugs triggered insanity and lurid crime sprees. The commission was told of an unfortunate Bengali man who brutally murdered his own family after an attack of "ganja mania." Another witness testified about a ruthless band of eleventh-century Persian warriors who would eat hashish and then commit

These tribes soon mastered the technique of smoking hash through long water pipes connected to a burning bowl made of animal horns.

Hemp Catches On

By the late nineteenth century, the use of hemp as an intoxicant was spreading to other parts of the world. North African tribes, introduced to hash by visiting Arabs, embraced it and explored ways to make smoking more enjoyable and social. These tribes soon mastered the technique of smoking hash through long water pipes connected to a burning bowl made of animal horns. Their indulgence became communal, with groups gathering in smoking circles. This was the genesis of silly pot party behavior.

Have a toke with your poke.

Two Plants in One

By the time botanists got around to classifying the plant, there was controversy. Carl Linnaeus named it *cannabis sativa* in 1753. But others in the horticultural world weren't satisfied, pointing out that there really were two types of cannabis. There was the plant known as hemp to North Americans and Europeans, and that other kind of plant, the one with the intoxicating belt. So they decided to add a designation for the more provocative hemp plant, naming it *cannabis indica*.

By dividing marijuana into two categories, botanists were making it official that cannabis is truly a Jeckyl

Tribal smokers sometimes amused themselves by seeing who could spit the most after taking mammoth, saliva-drying hits off the communal water pipe.

Napoleon's Nile army picked up the hash habit while on duty abroad and dutifully brought it home. By the mid-nineteenth century, bohemian enclaves were gathering to imbibe at discreet hashish clubs in Paris that served up gourmet meals with a hash jelly appetizer. Similar clubs sprung up in New York City and other urban zones across America.

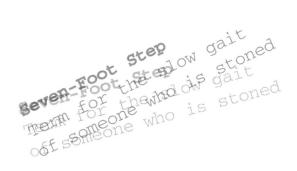

Seven-Foot Step
Term for the slow gait of someone who is stoned

Cannabis sativa L.

(1) Top of flowering male plant; (2) Top of female plant, with fruit;
(3) seedling; (4) leaflet from 11-parted leaf; (5) a staminate
inflorescence, with buds and mature male flower; (6) female flowers,
with stigmas and hairy bract; (7) fruit enclosed in hairy bract;
(8) fruit, side view; (9) fruit, bottom view; (10) glandular hair;
(11) glandular hair; (12) non-glandular hair with cystolith.

you lazy and forgetful. Contradictions abound. Early American marijuana critics charged that the weed caused insanity; during the same period, doctors were using marijuana to treat insanity. Marijuana smoking induces binge eating known as "the munchies"; meanwhile, Indian ascetics ingest hemp to prepare for fasting.

Virtually every culture has named it, from Scandinavians to Slavs, from Arabs to Anglo-Saxons. As an intoxicant, marijuana has been called everything from "Acapulco gold" to *zol*, the term given to a marijuana cigarette in South Africa. The Chinese call it *ma*. In other Asian cultures, it's referred to as the "increaser of pleasure," the "cementer of friendship," and the "exciter of desire." One of the earliest uses of marijuana in English refers to it as a "drug that brings false heart to the user."

and Hyde plant. Viewpoints about marijuana are passionate and extreme. Lighting up a joint is the path to ineffable pleasure for some; to others, it's the first step on the road to ruin. Marijuana makes you a red-hot musician, or it just makes

Pot and Religion

Some marijuana enthusiasts, perhaps seeking a divine thumbs-up for their pot habit, believe that there are marijuana references in the Bible. Mind you, there's nothing as blatant as an eleventh Commandment to "Go Forth and Bongeth." But the Bible contains several oblique references to mysterious herbs, spices, and burning rituals that sound suspiciously similar to how hash and hemp were used during that period.

Certainly there's proof that the Israelites knew of hemp at the time of the Bible. But hash and hemp don't play a major role in Christianity or Judaism. However, they do play a more high-profile role in other religious texts and customs.

The Indian spiritual books, called the Vedas, contain the story of Shiva, a spiritual-enlightenment deity in Hindu religion who was known as the "Lord of Bhang." *Bhang* is the Indian term for hash. According to the Vedas, Shiva wanders into a field after a family spat and takes cover under a hemp plant. He eats some of its leaves, which bring him comfort and refreshment. After the experience, he becomes a hemp missionary, spreading word of the plant's benefits to others. For Shiva followers, the hemp plant is a holy symbol of success and good fortune. During some rituals, it is a sin not to drink bhang.

Marijuana was also popular with some break-away sects. Tantric followers, who pursued ritualized sex as a means of attaining spiritual awakening, incorporated hash beverages and smoking into their sacred frolicking. This practice combined marijuana's psychoactive and sensory-stimulating effects. The Persian prophet Zaroaster, who was said to enter the world laughing around 500 B.C., promoted a substance called *haoma* that would help users obtain wisdom, success, and long life—even soul travel. The substance most likely was hash. In Africa, dagga cults believed hash was a god-given gift to the earth.

The most prominent religion today with marijuana as a major component is Rastafarianism, a religious-cultural movement with roots in 1930's Jamaica. Rastafarians believe that *ganja* is a sacred weed that is not only used in rituals but as a medicine as well. Popular reggae artists sing of the Rastafarian religion and their spiritual reverence for ganja, helping communicate the nature of the religion to a wide audience across the world.

The bad girl in all her glory.

Earning a Bad Name

Marijuana wasn't even "marijuana" in America until the 1920s. As Mexican slang for a hemp cigarette, "marijuana" is the name that stuck, mostly because it was the preferred choice of politicians, journalists, and others opposing it during this time. These anti-marijuana forces believed that by linking cannabis to the decadent ways of Mexican field workers, Americans would quickly grow to despise and fear it.

Shunned by the mainstream, early marijuana smokers clustered in bohemian enclaves, speaking a secret language to bond with others and exclude the unhip—and the cops. There are hundreds of ways to talk about marijuana without using the word. Marijuana smokers have answered to names such as "bushwacker," "hay burner," and "weed head." "Pot," another common name for marijuana, most likely came from the fact that marijuana was grown in flower pots during the 1940s. It was also commonly brewed in a pot as a tea. From pot comes "pot head," a frequent user of marijuana, and "potted," which means to be high. You could be potted but you could also be "wasted," "stoned," or just have a little "buzz." The herb itself has been called "gage," "gash," "giggle smoke," and "green griff," to name only a few. With such a large marijuana

> **"Pot," another common name for marijuana, most likely came from the fact that marijuana was grown in flower pots during the 1940s.**

> **Marijuana smokers were portrayed in newspapers and lurid pulp fiction books as lazy, degenerate, crazy, and, most often, foreign.**

vocabulary, choice of words is revealing. When someone talks about "dirt weed," you know it's bottom-barrel stuff that can't compare with a bud of potent "chronic." The herb itself has been rolled into cigarettes known as "joints," "reefers," "muggles," "goof butts," "doobies," "fatties," and "blunts"—a list that goes on and on.

The Marijuana Menace

Narcotics officers and lawmakers have their own terms for marijuana too, but they're less flattering. In the early part of the twentieth century, authorities aimed to outlaw the "marijuana menace" and stamp out the "loco weed." This period was critical for marijuana in America. The campaign was designed to generate public hysteria. Marijuana smokers were

portrayed in newspapers and lurid pulp fiction books as lazy, degenerate, crazy, and, most often, foreign. Marijuana addiction was seen as an outside problem threatening to corrupt Americans. Historians suggest that hidden racism was really behind political and legal efforts to wipe out marijuana use in America in the 1920s and 1930s. Most smokers at that time were black Americans or visiting Mexican laborers. Conspiracy theorists have other ideas. Some suggest that the liquor industry mounted the campaign, since

Americans who started lighting up reefers in the 1930s often talked about how it gave them confidence and a sense of well-being. That was a double-edged sword for a government trying to steer its way out of a depression. Poor Americans might smoke reefers and suddenly imagine they were entitled to more in life, threatening the country's stability. On the other hand, good reefer might make the masses content to settle for less.

The idea that marijuana smoking might encourage counterproductive attitudes in America's work force was eloquently stated in a short story by Terry Southern called "Red Dirt Marijuana." In the story, an experienced marijuana smoker tells a young boy why he believes marijuana is illegal: "It ain't because it makes young boys like you sick, I tell you that much... it's cause man see too much when he git high, that's why. He see right through ever'thing... Shoot, ever'body git high, wouldn't be nobody git up an' feed the chickens!"

marijuana was a cheaper thrill than another vice—alcohol, which was once again socially acceptable following the repeal of Prohibition. Others suggest that the government was moving to protect the interests of a few large companies who made wood, paper, and plastic products that competed with hemp.

> **"It ain't because it makes young boys like you sick, I tell you that much...it's cause man see too much when he git high, that's why. He see right through ever'thing... Shoot, ever'body git high, wouldn't be nobody git up an' feed the chickens!"**
> **—"Red Dirt Marijuana" by Terry Southern**

> **When Reagan launched the war on drugs in a 1982 speech, marijuana was the only drug he mentioned by name.**

No matter the motivation, marijuana was first restricted at the federal level with the Marijuana Tax Act of 1937. It was now illegal to use marijuana—in the eyes of the Treasury Department. While marijuana offenses were considered tax violations, they could still get you serious prison time—up to five years. Marijuana laws have grown more severe in passing years. There was a brief respite during the stoner heyday of the 1970s. Once the haze cleared, however, legalization efforts went up in smoke during the 1980s under Ronald Reagan's "zero-tolerance" war on drugs. In fact, when Reagan launched the war on drugs in a 1982 speech, marijuana was the only drug he mentioned by name.

This harsh political and legal climate endures, but smokers keep lighting up. Marijuana use caught hold in America during the 1960s, when widespread experimentation spread to the biggest enclave in America: the college campus. Marijuana's mild euphoric effects meshed perfectly with the mind-expanding curiosities of rebellious young Americans looking for safe thrills. By 1972, it was estimated that 24 million Americans had used it. That figure is now up to 70 million. Marijuana use has spread to all parts of society, from weary office workers to grandmothers toking up to stave off the effects of cancer treatments.

Critical Period

The marijuana plant is entering a crucial time in its history. Still popular as a recreational drug, marijuana is also experiencing a resurgence in its more sober historical applications. Activists are campaigning at federal and state levels to legalize it for a variety of medical uses, most notably to ease the nausea of

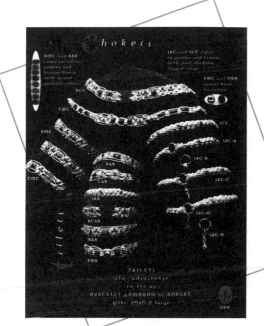

Hip hemp jewelry.

lotion and hair products. Major retailers, such as the Body Shop, have boldly placed marijuana leaves on their front windows to promote their line of hemp skin-care products. Some visionaries are touting hemp as a substitute for plastic goods and even as an energy source.

Strangely enough, hemp is also turning up at the dinner table, in another resurgence of a past application. For years, hemp seed was pressed into cooking oil. It was also fed to birds as a nutritional snack that made their coats fluffier and coaxed them to sing in a pleasing, full-throated style. Shoppers now find hemp listed in the ingredients of beer, wine, and pretzels. You say hemp, but some people still say marijuana. Efforts to expand the hemp market have been met strongly by the anti-drug movement. Pity hemp—the straight-A student mistakenly tarnished with the shameful reputation of a delinquent sibling.

chemotherapy patients and the "wasting-away" syndrome of AIDS sufferers. Others are campaigning to use it to treat glaucoma and arthritis.

Meanwhile, hemp is suddenly hip. A major effort is underway to revive hemp in America, harkening to a simpler time before the plant got all mixed up with marijuana. Hemp merchandise is showing up in mainstream malls in the form of clothes and more exotic fare such as body

Pity hemp—the straight-A student mistakenly tarnished with the shameful reputation of a delinquent sibling.

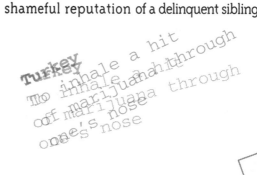

Turkey
To inhale a hit
off marijuana through
one's nose

If hemp does make it all the way back, it will revive a once-starring role for the almost forgotten fiber. Hemp once played a pivotal role in North America and Europe during the age of exploration. In the sixteenth and seventeenth centuries, when world power was determined by naval domination, hemp was the fabric of choice for maritime sails and rope. Fleets depended on quality hemp, and wars were fought to protect supply lines. Hemp rope was coveted because it was so strong. Because of this quality, it was widely used as a noose, leading to terms such as "hempen necklace" and "hempen necktie." An early American expression, "All right on the hemp," meant that you were dead sure about something.

The value of hemp was not lost on American colonialists. They were ordered to grow it as a way of building a foundation for independence. Not growing hemp could land a farmer in jail. Echoing that patriotism, American farmers were urged to plant a "Hemp for Victory" crop during World War II in order to produce enough hemp fiber to supply the military effort.

Hemp was a back-breaking, labor-intensive crop, and one that American farmers weren't particularly adept at growing. American hemp was inferior to hemp grown in Europe and Russia. New equipment was developed for use in America in the 1930s that would make hemp processing easier and profitable. However, a government-backed anti-marijuana effort crushed any hope of a hemp comeback.

Bush Tea
Marijuana tea

A Shadow Culture

While it's possible to track the hemp economy, marijuana is never officially listed as part of a nation's fiscal activity. But marijuana has generated a sizable market-place of its own, involving growers, dealers, and buyers.

The trippiest triangle in California.

They trade in not only marijuana but related products, from growing supplies and stash boxes to bongs and rolling papers. It's a marketplace that has grown more sophisticated through the years. Young entrepreneurs have spruced up the old head shop by opening combination marijuana boutiques and hemp food cafes. Bongs, once marketed as throw-away plastic accessories, are now sold as one-of-a-kind art items, with the expected higher prices.

While American farmers grew inferior hemp, they've excelled with marijuana. American growers have led the way as pot has soared to a new level of complexity.

Like mad scientists with green thumbs, growers have cross-bred seeds to adjust for a plant's potency, perfecting a killer bud from unfertilized females called "sinsemilla."

Sinsemilla in America began in select growing regions. The Emerald Triangle area of Northern California is to sinsemilla as Napa Valley is to wine. In a state famed for its agricultural output, marijuana quickly became California's biggest cash crop. It is also America's richest crop. High-quality marijuana is now grown in every state. It is painstakingly bred by connoisseurs who sample buds like wine lovers to evaluate their bouquet, physical appearance, taste, potency, and the depths of the resulting high. Even with diligent federal efforts to eradicate the U.S. marijuana crop, growers have survived by being industrious and adaptive, enduring much like the plant itself in the wild.

A presidential endorsement straight from the mouth of G.W.

I Want to Take You Higher

The high from marijuana is very subjective. Many first-time users report no reaction at all. When marijuana smokers are asked to recall the first time they got high, most will divide the answer into two parts: the first time they smoked pot, and the first time they caught a buzz. Users praise pot for promoting a sense of well-being and increasing sensory perceptions. Being high enriches simple pleasures, such as eating, sex, or listening to music. It may bring about insights and spiritual enlightenment, or it may simply impair driving skills or make people forget the subject of conversations they've just started.

Marijuana has certainly had a profound effect upon American culture. It paved the way for the creation of jazz music in New Orleans by inspiring Storyville musicians to experiment with new musical phrases and syncopation. Long before Clinton swallowed the truth with his "I didn't inhale" line in 1992, America's first president, George Washington, openly

Washington even took pains to separate male and female hemp plants, a method of improving a crop's psychoactive potency.

Weed: A Rare Batch
Stash st107
Classic Jazz Vocals

welcome plate of munchies by Martha Washington.

Writers from Homer to playwright Neil Simon have included references to marijuana in their works. Some, like French Romantics and, later, American Beats, smoked it for artistic inspiration. Marijuana has been celebrated in song by musicians ranging from jazz vipers, including Cab Calloway and Louis Armstrong, to modern pop stars, such as the Black Crowes and Cypress Hill.

Marijuana has made it to the big screen and the little screen. It was smoked up in mass quantities by the super-buzzed comedy duo Cheech and Chong in the 1970s. More recently, it was used matter-of-factly by Arliss, the duplicitous sports agent of HBO's comedy series. Meanwhile, marijuana is now a featured player in cyberspace, where a network of cannabis-related sites offer everything from vital medical information and brownie recipes to instructions for pot games and home-growing tips.

talked about tending to his hemp garden, and not very well at that. Washington grew hemp for its useful fiber, but gave indications that he expanded his garden to include more intoxicating varieties of the plant. Washington even took pains to separate male and female hemp plants, a method of improving a crop's psychoactive potency. In his book *Mason & Dixon*, author Thomas Pynchon conjures up a scene where the father of our country smokes a bowl of hemp with the two famous surveyors after whom the book is titled. The stoned trio is then served a

Pancho Villa to troops: "Toke up and charge!"

A Role at Work

While the prevailing image of a pot head is one who sits around and munches out while pondering his ash-strewn naval, marijuana has, in fact, woven itself into the fabric of the workplace. For centuries, soldiers have taken it to war. Zulu warriors in Africa were observed toking up before battle to boost their courage. Pancho Villa's revolutionary army was probably the first documented band of warriors to go to battle while

stoned. A half century later, American GIs would also seek solace in a marijuana high while fighting in Vietnam.

Marijuana has proven to be the downfall of some classes of workers, from politicians to professional sports stars. The public continues to show less tolerance for pot use among its more high-profile citizens. For others, including Indian laborers under British rule, Mexican farm workers at the turn of the century in America, and, more recently, bored office workers, marijuana has provided relief from tedium and fatigue.

The Science of Marijuana

Marijuana has been at the heart of heated scientific debate for decades. Research shows that the human brain has specific receptors for THC in a high-density region known as the hippocampus, which plays a role in cognition and motor function. Other parts of the brain bond with THC as well, including regions related to sensory awareness. Beyond these basic facts, controversy reigns as to the health and psychological consequences of marijuana use. Dozens of unsuspecting laboratory animals have been stoned in the name of science, from baboons to bats, in the search for answers about the weed's mysterious and complex effects upon people. Human volunteers have gotten buzzed in the lab as well. One seemingly obvious study set out to determine if stoned subjects would drink more chocolate milkshakes than straight subjects. The results were as expected.

One seemingly obvious study set out to determine if stoned subjects would drink more chocolate milkshakes than straight subjects. The results were as expected.

The Battle of Perception

Against this backdrop of scientific research, politicians, law enforcement officials, and advocacy groups continue to voice opinions about the marijuana plant. American anti-drug forces now battle a three-headed drug menace in marijuana: hemp advocates, medicinal proponents, and those fighting for the right to light up. Despite spending billions to convince Americans of the evils of marijuana, the federal government still faces a public that doesn't view it as harmful as other illegal drugs, such as heroin or cocaine. At a 1995 conference sponsored by the National Institute on Drug Abuse, then drug czar Lee Brown noted that one of the biggest challenges facing anti-marijuana efforts was changing the public's perception. His aim was to silence any opposition to the government's "no tolerance" policy on marijuana, and he boldly told the conference gathering, "We who have access to the most accurate and advanced information should be driving the discussion about finding solutions to the drug problem, not those with the least knowledge who often seem to have the most to say."

Caught in the middle of all this hot air is the plant itself. Maybe what is needed is not less talk, as Brown suggests, but more. How much influence has marijuana really had in America? It was around when jazz was born, and many other artistic endeavors have been nurtured by marijuana smoking. Marijuana continues to have a profound effect upon the daily lives of Americans. It's still the most frequently detected banned substance among drug-tested American workers. The marijuana business is a black market industry, but one that has a great impact on the American economy. Consider this: The 1970s saw a rise in convenience stores alongside a similar rise in marijuana smoking during a period of relaxed marijuana enforcement. Coincidence? As any munchie-crazed stoner can tell you, the convenience store is nirvana—it's loaded with easily accessible junk food. Stoners pump up profits at convenience stores. How many other economic trends have been fueled by marijuana use?

Where is it all going? Will hemp become a world-saving miracle crop? Will American tokers one day be able to walk into a supermarket and buy a pack of joints as naturally as picking up a gallon of milk? Will former American tobacco farmers rebound with a hemp crop? Will it become common for doctors to send patients to pharmacies to pick up their marijuana medicine? Or will the vice tighten even more around marijuana, hemp, and hash? The fate of the marijuana plant, much like the way it reproduces, is up in the air.

The 1970s saw a rise in convenience stores alongside a similar rise in marijuana smoking during a period of relaxed marijuana enforcement. Coincidence?

Honey Blunts
Marijuana cigars sealed
with sweet honey

marijuana & society

"book 'em, dano"

the first law regulating marijuana in America was passed by the Virginia Assembly in 1619. Far from outlawing marijuana, colonial lawmakers were instead urgently ordering Americans to plant a homegrown crop. No one was promoting recreational pleasures, though. Most farmers had never heard of anyone smoking the plant they knew as hemp, much less tried it themselves for kicks. If anyone had suggested it, it would have seemed as preposterous to them as smoking an ear of corn. They were, after all, growing hemp for its sturdy stalk. It was harvested and processed to make sails, rigging, and ship caulking, as well as clothing. The hemp crop was so vital that residents of Virginia, Pennsylvania, and Maryland were allowed to use it as money—a law passed to stimulate its cultivation.

The hemp crop was so vital that residents of Virginia, Pennsylvania, and Maryland were allowed to use it as money—a law passed to stimulate its cultivation.

The American hemp market faded away with slumping demand after the Civil War. By the time hemp surged back into public view, it was under less favorable circumstances. By 1910, Americans began hearing about a new drug menace—the smoking of the flowering tops and leaves of the once-benevolent hemp plant. This time, however, hemp was going by a new name: "marijuana."

27

c h chapter Two o
apter c
p t e r

25¢ Unmasking a Vicious Racket

AN ORIGINAL PUBLICATION

Early Drug Problems

America's first drug problems had nothing to do with hemp or marijuana. Even though it grew wild in many states, it wouldn't be until the 1960s that marijuana use became widespread in America.

However, at the turn of the century, Americans were very familiar with narcotics such as morphine and opium. America had hundreds of morphine addicts, hooked as a result of the Civil War, when it was used as a miracle pain reliever on the battlefield. Morphine addiction became known as the "soldier's disease." In addition, myriad peddlers were hawking secret potions that contained heavy doses of morphine—although never labeled as such. These popular remedies turned scores of patients looking for miracle cures into unsuspecting morphine addicts.

The first step taken by the United States to control its drug problem was the Pure Food and Drug Act of 1906. This law aimed to restrict elixir peddlers by declaring that drugs could be sold only by prescription, and that all drug distributors be government licensed. The bill had much greater significance. It established the government as watchdog over all the drugs and medications Americans took to make themselves feel better. These powers were broadened with the Harrison Tax Act of 1914, which made the "nonmedical use" of opium, morphine, and cocaine a crime.

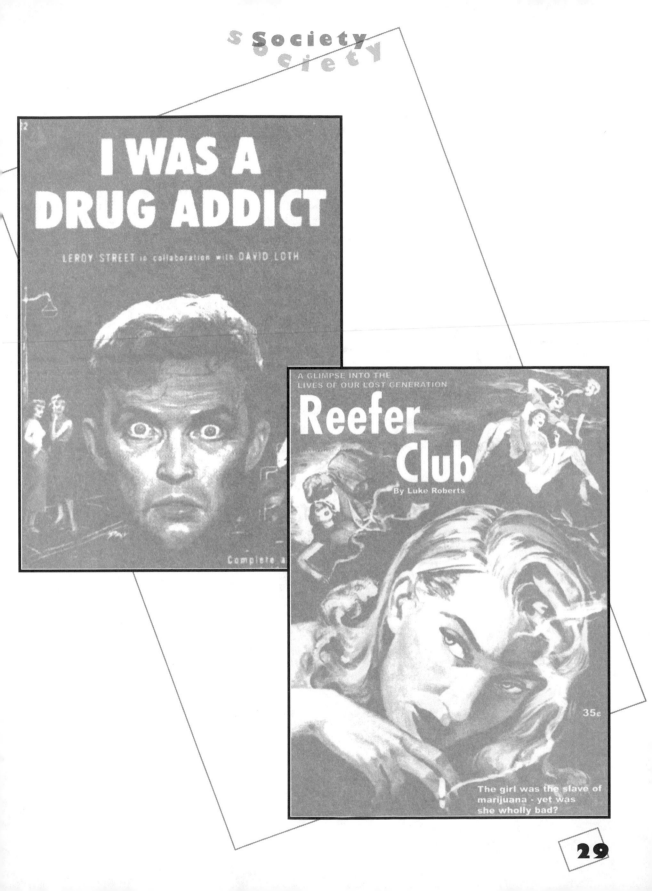

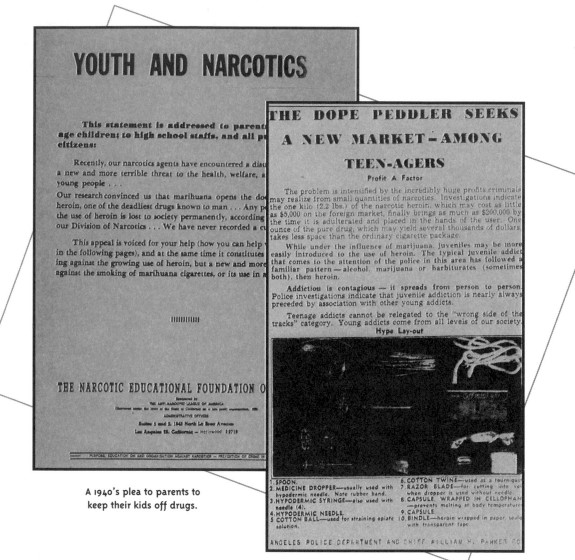

A 1940's plea to parents to keep their kids off drugs.

Because this was a tax act, enforcement fell to the Treasury Department. The first prohibition of narcotics in the United States essentially made drug use a crime of tax evasion, a pattern that followed with the Marijuana Tax Act of 1937.

The circumstances surrounding the initial federal ban on marijuana are critical because its effects are still felt today. By the time the federal government stepped in, a sizable anti-marijuana coalition was already hard at work

Zealous journalists, politicians, and police forces
spoke out against "hemp"
smokers as if the very fate of
the country were hanging in
the balance. The overall goal
was to make the public
believe that marijuana use
would turn people into
insane criminals.

convincing the public of the evils of this
new and deadly form of drug abuse.
Lawmakers joined the crusade, expressing
their outrage and then voting accordingly
to pass anti-marijuana laws in several
states and cities—even though marijuana
smokers were scarce in early twentieth-
century America. Isolated groups of
smokers were gathering around the
campfire at Mexican labor camps in the
West and South or huddling up in hash
dens in New Orleans, New York, and other
urban bohemian enclaves. Nevertheless,
zealous journalists, politicians, and police
forces spoke out against "hemp" smokers
as if the very fate of the country were
hanging in the balance. Their rhetoric was
characterized by hype and the telling of
exotic myths. The overall goal was to make
the public believe that marijuana use
would turn people into insane criminals.

Hidden Racism

There are many theories as to why
marijuana was considered such a threat.
Some point to the 1898 seizure of eight
hundred thousand acres of timberland
belonging to William Randolph Hearst by
Pancho Villa's pot-smoking army as the
underlying cause for much of the yellow
journalism scripted against marijuana.
However, the most reasonable explanation
for early prohibition campaigns is
suggested from research conducted by
professors Richard Bonnie and Charles
Whitebread in their article "The Forbidden
Fruit and the Tree of Knowledge: An
Inquiry into the Legal History of American
Marijuana Prohibition," which was
published in the Virginia Law Review in
October 1970. They concluded that early
marijuana muckrakers were motivated by
racial prejudice.

Early hemp drug use in America was tied
to Mexican field workers flooding the
country after the turmoil of the Mexican
Revolution of 1910. Quite naturally for

A Mexican peddler arrested by California narcotic inspectors, with a bale of marijuana, or Indian hemp. Cigarettes are made from leaves and flowers

WIPING OUT A CITY-GROWN PATCH OF MARIJUANA
A police emergency squad eradicating a patch of the drug-producing plants from a vacant lot in Astoria, N. Y. Its resemblance to common weeds often makes hemp hard to iden...

were cloaked in anti-immigration sentiment. For example, when Montana held hearings to ban it in 1929, a Dr. Fred Fulsher of Mineral County testified, "When some beet field peon takes a few rares of this stuff, he thinks he has just been elected president of Mexico so he starts out to execute all of his political enemies."

Lurid headlines began appearing around the country, tying marijuana use to horrible sexual perversions and brutal crime sprees. An article in *The American Mercury* in 1935 played up racial fears with a story that ran under the bold headline "The Marijuana Menace." It described the

them, they brought along marijuana, consumed as a relaxing smoke after a hard day in the field. This was as routine for them as workers today slugging back a happy-hour cocktail. At the same time, Caribbean sailors coming ashore in the Gulf of Mexico port cities also brought their stash, intending to spice up shore leave. These two groups introduced Americans to the recreational possibilities of the hemp plant.

One of the country's first anti-marijuana laws was passed in 1914 in El Paso, Texas. By 1931, 21 states banned its use, relying on the testimony of so-called marijuana experts who warned of its perilous social consequences. Early state bans of marijuana

> **Lurid headlines began appearing around the country, tying marijuana use to horrible sexual perversions and brutal crime sprees.**

Some of the marijuana captured in a raid. The cigarettes often cost several dollars each

describes marijuana as "a most pernicious and widely used drug...Its inhalation may produce criminal insanity and cause juvenile delinquency." Provocative words such as "pernicious" and "menace" were favorites among anti-marijuana crusaders.

In a story about the National Congress of Parents and Teachers meeting in May 1937, marijuana was singled out in a strongly worded headline: "War on Marijuana Urged on Parents." A U.S. Federal Bureau of Narcotics officer warned the gathering that marijuana is a "most pernicious drug" that provokes numerous sex crimes. Buried further down in the story are speakers with other notions about what temptations might be threatening America's youth. They cautioned against alcohol, warning parents and teachers about the "corruption of the tavern." But those kinds of claims were not big news. Marijuana was the exotic new villain, commanding headlines.

"Harlemites" who smoked the weed as an aphrodisiac: "A Negro was brought to a New York hospital because he had run after and threatened two women in the street while under the influence of reefers; he said he had seen in his reefer dream 'a bunch of naked wimmin, some of 'em in bed, black an' white together like dey was expectin' men.'" Even the relatively staid *New York Times* was not immune from introducing this slant into their marijuana coverage. It featured a 1937 article headlined "Marijuana Spreads Its Web on America." The account

The roots of reefer madness: Harry Anslinger's essay "Assassin of Youth."

Marijuana: Assassin of Youth

The government official most responsible for creating anti-marijuana hysteria in America is Harry Anslinger. Like his bureaucratic peer at the Federal Bureau of Investigation, J. Edgar Hoover, Anslinger held a similar long-term reign as head of the Federal Bureau of Narcotics. Anslinger took over as director of the FBN in 1930 and served through five administrations until 1962, when President Kennedy forced him out. While others certainly had a hand in stirring up public fervor against the evil

A weed that grows wild throughout the country is making dope addicts of thousands of young people

BY H. J. ANSLINGER

U. S. Commissioner of Narcotics

WITH COURTNEY RYLEY COOPER

Anslinger's onslaught of anti-marijuana rhetoric was shrewd and effective. Like a modern-day talk-show host, Anslinger grabbed the public's attention by illustrating a social issue with shocking stories of real people. Anslinger's influential speeches and writings were high on human drama and vague on specifics. He told of the horrors of innocent youths driven insane by smoking a single reefer, and wayward kids who would slay their entire family after a few puffs. His masterful work, where his tabloid skills are fully evident, is the sensational essay "Assassin of Youth." This combative plea to arouse public outrage over marijuana use

weed, Anslinger's role was profound and enduring.

Once Prohibition ended, federal agents who had formerly chased after bootleggers found a convenient new foe in reefer heads. To convince the public of the evils of a substance that most Americans couldn't identify, Anslinger waged a tireless public relations campaign. He railed against marijuana with unrelenting venom, portraying it as a deadly menace that was corrupting American youth and weakening the foundation of American society. Anslinger also believed in treating drug addicts as criminals and locking them in jails, dismissing the alternative of treatment centers by sarcastically calling them "barrooms for addicts."

Harry Anslinger took over as director of the FBN in 1930 and served through five administrations until 1962, when President Kennedy forced him out. While others certainly had a hand in stirring up public fervor against the evil weed, Anslinger's role was profound and enduring.

Pot's public enemy #1: Harry Anslinger.

ran in general interest magazines and was published as a pulp fiction book. For most Americans, Anslinger's perspective provided their only knowledge of the marijuana experience. "Assassin of Youth" begins with a noir, punchy crime-scene description that could conclude with probably dozens of social ills as the cause. In this case, the villain is an evil weed: "The sprawled body of a young girl lay crushed on the sidewalk the other day after a plunge from the fifth story of a Chicago apartment house. Everyone called it suicide, but actually, it was murder. The killer was a narcotic known to America as marijuana, and to history as hashish. It is a narcotic used in the form of cigarettes,

comparatively new to the United States and as dangerous as a coiled rattlesnake."

The reptilian analogy is pretty tame for what comes next. Anslinger blames marijuana for countless "murders, suicides, robberies, criminal assaults, holdups, burglaries and deeds of maniacal insanity," all of which he describes in graphic detail. Eventually, Anslinger returns to the story of that "suicidal" young girl. He paints a picture of her demise for the public, cleverly avoiding specifics so parents everywhere could imagine that it was their own innocent child. Feeling pressure from too much school work, the girl gathers with friends to seek solace by smoking a cigarette of the "homemade type": "The results were weird. Some of the party went into paroxysms of laughter; every remark, no matter how silly, seemed excruciatingly funny. Others of mediocre musical ability became almost expert; the piano dinned constantly...As one youngster expressed it, he 'could see through stone walls.'" Eventually, after similar gatherings, Anslinger describes how the girl "walked to the window and leaped to her death."

Marijuana Mythology

Sensational stories about the dangers of marijuana have been critical weapons in the fight against its use. A favorite myth was the story of the *haschischin*, a band of hash-crazed Persian killers from the eleventh century. Federal Bureau of Narcotics Director Harry Anslinger frequently cited this Persian order as an example of how marijuana and hash could turn people into murderous lunatics. The story had a bonus effect: By connecting hash and marijuana use to Arabia, Anslinger linked it with a culture Americans considered mysterious and dangerous. It was an effective ploy to make Americans fearful of using it and to recruit them as eager allies in the fight against it. A 1936 article in *Popular Science Monthly* called hash the "'emerald green' drug of the Arabs."

Marijuana and hash excesses were related to other exotic cultures as well. Americans were told that the term "running amok" described Malay natives who fell under the influence of hashish and committed "violent and bloody deeds." An article in *Popular Science Monthly* of 1936 told the story: "In Malay, where it is eaten as hashish, the murderous frenzy in which the native dashes with a weapon into a crowd screaming, 'Amok! Amok!' (Kill! Kill!) is due to the drug, according to some travelers." Just which travelers is never stated.

Anslinger's stories portrayed villains such as the hot-tamale salesman in Birmingham, Alabama, described in "Assassin of Youth," who had a side business of pushing reefers to school kids. But Anslinger preferred more dramatic fare. One of his classic tales is the 1933 family tragedy in Tampa, Florida, where a young man named Victor Licata axed his parents, two brothers, and a sister to death. Because he told police he had been smoking marijuana, blaring newspaper headlines following the murder talked of a "crazed youth" driven mad by the "poisonous mind-wrecking weed." Later, however, it was revealed that Victor had a history of psychosis. He was eventually declared insane. That never stopped Anslinger from featuring the Licata case as a prime example of the menace of marijuana.

Vital questions asked by
modern youth are answered
by Los Angeles
authorities in this--

Report on Narcotics

- Is there a road back?
- Might I get "hooked"?

- Is addiction a respecter of persons?
- Marijuana—as dangerous as heroin?
- Why does the "stuff" allure?
- Who are the real "pushers"?

Marijuana once again makes the headlines in this piece of 1940's government propaganda.

Pot Propaganda

Anslinger wasn't fighting marijuana alone. He was joined in his crusade by a shrill chorus of marijuana maligners including journalists, scientists, and law enforcement officers who also copied his hyperbolic style. Doctor Pablo Wolff, for example, published a report in 1949 that described the unfortunate marijuana user as someone who is "subjugated by this weed, messenger of a false happiness, panderer to a treacherous love, which can provide superhuman enjoyment and misery...and changes thousands of persons into nothing more than human scum." Ouch.

Typical frenzied newspaper accounts include a headline in the *Los Angeles Examiner* of 1933 that warned "Deadly Marijuana Dope Plant Ready for Harvest That Means Enslavement of California Children." A 1936 *Popular Science Monthly* article ran under the panic-inducing headline "Uncle Sam Fights New Drug Menace...Marijuana." The article pointed out that whenever police were confronted with a "particularly horrible crime... especially one pointing to perversion,"

Reagan Aide: Pot Can Make You Gay

Senior presidential aides looked on White House drug adviser Carlton E. Turner as a nattily dressed functionary with zero ~~~~ He ~~~~ his time ~~~~ to be something that follows along from their marijuana use," says Turner, who is convinced that the drugs come first, the homosexuality sec~~~~ to AIDS, a dise~~~~ stroys the im~~~~ "No one is saying th~~~~ juana will *cause* A~~~~ says, but he argues~~~~

New government study finds pot can make you say stupid things.

the cops first questioned marijuana smokers. An article in *Scientific American* in 1938 labeled marijuana as more dangerous than heroin or cocaine.

Sensational claims about marijuana haven't faded away. In 1981, for example, *Reader's Digest* launched an explosive three-part series called "Marijuana Alerts." The final installment, "The Devastation of Personality," compares a chronic marijuana user unfavorably to the heavy drinker, who sobers up nicely and "becomes himself again." Meanwhile, the article states, the pot head remains in a chronic "state of subacute intoxication." Echoing Anslinger's use of human drama, the article quotes a lost 16-year-old boy who says, "I'm like an empty shell. There is nothing left

In 1986, Carlton Turner, serving as President Reagan's drug advisor, suggested that marijuana would make you gay. Turner based his conclusion on visits to drug-treatment centers where he found a high percentage of homosexual patients.

that I like about myself. And pot did it." The article concludes with comments by Carlton Turner, the former director of the government's marijuana research farm in Mississippi, who claims that pot smoking in America threatens the "future of our families and our nation."

Scary rumors about the grotesque consequences of pot smoking, including that it would cause men to grow breasts, have been ideas floated in recent times. In 1986, Carlton Turner, serving as President Reagan's drug advisor, suggested that marijuana would make you gay. Turner based his conclusion on visits to drug-treatment centers where he found a high percentage of homosexual patients. "It seems to be something that follows along from their marijuana use," Turner concluded.

The Feds Take Action

With the seeds for public distrust of marijuana firmly planted, federal lawmakers moved to ban its use. At a congressional hearing, a mild protest to the proposed law was voiced by an industry representative who wanted to make sure it wouldn't affect the supply of hemp bird seeds. His fears were eased. But not so for the American Medical Association's legislative counsel, William Woodward, who testified that there was no evidence that marijuana use was harmful. He was chastised by one congressman and scolded, "Doctor, if you can't say something good about what we're trying to do, why don't you go home."

The first federal marijuana prohibition was passed on August 2, 1937. When the bill came before the House, it was debated for all of 90 seconds. From published testimony it's clear most lawmakers didn't know what they were voting on. The Marijuana Tax Act of 1937 imposed penalties that included a $2,000 fine and up to five years in jail. Soon after the bill was passed, Samuel Caldwell became the first marijuana felon, a dealer sentenced to four years of hard labor at Leavenworth Penitentiary.

Following the tax act, marijuana laws grew more oppressive—a trend that remained until the 1970s. The Boggs Act of 1951, followed by the Narcotics Control Act of 1956, made marijuana a hard drug, equating penalties for its use with that of heroin and cocaine. States mirrored the federal bills with strict drug-control laws of their own, sometimes going to extremes. In Louisiana, first-time offenders could get a virtual life sentence of 99 years. In many states, murderers

In 1969, federal lawmakers passed the Dangerous Substances Act... Marijuana received the most restrictive designation, meaning it had no medical use and a high potential for abuse, putting it on par with drugs such as LSD, heroin, and peyote.

were serving less time than marijuana tokers, a judicial inequity that persists today.

Emerging scientific evidence that marijuana wasn't as dangerous as other hard drugs didn't stop anti-marijuana forces. They introduced the argument that marijuana should be outlawed because it was the steppingstone to harder drugs. That spin swayed lawmakers, who heaped further penalties on the marijuana-smoking community. In 1969, federal lawmakers passed the Dangerous Substances Act. This law classified all drugs according to "schedules" of their potential for abuse and medical use. Marijuana received the most restrictive designation, meaning it had no medical use and a high potential for abuse, putting it on par with drugs such as LSD, heroin, and peyote. The bill outlawed pot for all uses, including as a medicine.

Brief Window of Opportunity

The 1970s provided a short-lived trend toward more lenient restrictions on marijuana use. Eleven states decriminalized marijuana during this time while others eased off from harsh penalties. Even the Federal Drug Enforcement Agency was

swept up in the movement, suggesting in 1974 that decriminalization of marijuana was an idea worth considering.

A driving force behind this shift was that scores of Americans were trying pot. They could rely on firsthand knowledge of the drug's effects and consequences. It's estimated that 8 million Americans were using marijuana with some frequency in 1972, while 24 million had tried it. Sociologist Alfred Lindesmith of the University of Indiana warned parents somewhat sarcastically in a magazine article that "if a kid goes to college these days and never develops an interest in marijuana, he's got a problem and you should worry about it. He may be a loner and not accepted by his peers."

Another factor in this trend was that the prevailing social attitude was one of tolerance and exploration. It was popular to "question authority" and challenge old ideas—all within reason, of course. Americans experimented with alternative forms of religion, exercise, and medicine. They shopped for health foods. Streakers were bold heroes, while sex swingers frolicked in the normally button-down suburbs. Psychedelic fashions hung on

department store racks. As part of this wide-scale burst of freedom, marijuana and other party drugs were just another sign that times were changing.

Pro-marijuana rallies featured the smell of pot smoke wafting through the air, transforming efforts to roll back marijuana laws into public celebrations. Police officers began looking the other way when tokers lit up. When they didn't, pot heads could always turn to groups such as Free Weed, a San Francisco firm formed in 1970 that offered marijuana users a type of insurance against being busted. For 50 bucks a year, smokers were promised $1,500 in legal defense help if ever arrested for marijuana use. The group claimed five hundred members, resulting in a tidy profit for the three founders—except that one wasn't around to collect his earnings; he was serving time in a Canadian jail for marijuana possession.

It was still risky to take a pro-pot stance. In 1967, for example, Dr. James Goddard, head of the Food and Drug Administration, created a stir when he said that he didn't think that marijuana was any more dangerous than alcohol. Goddard responded to subsequent criticism, including some requests for his resignation, by pointing out that many people weren't aware of the dangers of alcohol.

Nixon: Friend or Foe?

In 1972, a commission appointed by President Nixon to evaluate the marijuana question came to the bold conclusion that it should be legalized for personal use. The National Commission on Marijuana and Drug Abuse, headed by former Pennsylvania Governor Raymond Shafer, wrote, "We believe that the criminal law is too harsh a tool to apply to personal possession even in the effort to discourage use...The actual and potential harm of use of the drug is not great enough to justify intrusion by the criminal law into private behavior."

Stating that the "evils" of marijuana are based "much more on fantasy than on proven fact," the commission concluded that marijuana was not physically addictive and did not lead to crime. It concluded that intermittent use did not pose a physical or psychological threat to users. The commission was wrong with one prediction, however, stating that the present interest in marijuana was "transient" and would "diminish in time of its own accord." While the commission's report was published, the recommendations were never implemented by the government.

Have You Raised a Pot Head?

In an effort to stamp out marijuana use among teens in Utah, a 60-page pamphlet—featuring a personal letter from Senator Orrin Hatch—was distributed by the Salt Lake Education Foundation to school age children in 1997. Between several color pictures of joints, hemp plants, and distraught-looking teenagers, are anecdotes of children's lives gone sour once they become regular users of the evil weed. A plan of attack is laid out for parents to follow, complete with a guide to medical, behavioral, and social signs that indicate their children may be "addicted" to marijuana.

Besides some typical teenage behaviors, such as avoiding one's parents, authorities in Utah claim that an interest in "Ras Tafari" religion is a sign that your child is smoking pot. Another red flag is a type of rebellious behavior described as "à la James Dean." The topper, however, is that marijuana use is said to lead to an "excessive preoccupation with social causes, race relations, environmental issues, etc."

Searching through your child's possessions is apparently acceptable, as the pamphlet guides the parent to sift through their children's belongings, looking out for eye drops, incense, and cough medicine—sure signs you've raised a pot head.

Partnership for a Drug-Free America

"ANY WAY YOU CAN TALK" :30

DECC-4349

DAD: Son…

(SFX: DAD CRACKING KNUCKLES)

Your mother and I have to talk to you.

MOM: It's important.

DAD: Marijuana.

(SFX: MOM SETTING DOWN BOOM BOX)

(SFX: DAD EXHALING)

(SFX: RAP MUSIC CLICK ON)

DAD RAPS: The wacky weed, it is bad.

Of this I know,

believe your dad. Remember this, it's your decision,

but marijuana can lead to prison.

ANNCR VO: Any way you choose…

DAD: Huh!
ANNCR VO: …to talk with your kids about drugs is a good way.

1-800-729-6686
Partnership for a Drug-Free America

Call for your free brochure.

Drug Czar Barry McCaffrey: making sure Bill doesn't inhale.

The War on Marijuana

The rise of vocal parent groups speaking out against drugs, as well as Ronald Reagan moving into the White House in 1980, signaled the end of America's incipient pot party. Reagan may have been acting on personal experience. His own daughter, Patti Davis, was a renegade hippie known for just saying yes to marijuana a few times.

The early 1980s saw the launch of an enduring anti-marijuana campaign waged by narcotics officers, bureaucrats, politicians, and anti-drug citizen groups.

Targeting marijuana and other illegal substances, the war on drugs features commando eradication programs and publicity campaigns laded with military metaphors. The campaign focuses on military codes of discipline, including "zero tolerance," mandatory prison sentencing, and an aggressive property seizure policy that resembles armies and their quest for spoils. The good fight against marijuana is fittingly being waged under President Bill Clinton by a lifelong soldier: General Barry McCaffrey, a former West Point Cadet who had tours in Vietnam and Iraq, took the position as drug czar in 1996. As director of the Office of National Drug Control Policy, McCaffrey announced a major anti-drug publicity blitz that makes marijuna use a prime target. It's a campaign waged by government groups as well as private agencies such as the Partnership for a Drug Free America.

The Partnership has orchestrated the most expensive public service campaign in history, topping $2.8 billion by the end of 1997, with much of that being spent to teach kids about the dangers of marijuana use. With support from two hundred corporations and an additional $200 million from the federal government, the Partnership launched a series of anti-drug

(Left) This ad from Partnership features a father who resorts to rapping in order to communicate with his son.

commercials produced to counter marijuana's resurgent popularity. "A lot of hippie imagery was coming back in; you could see that happening in fashion with the clothing," says Ginna Marston, the executive vice president of the Partnership for a Drug-Free America. "Popular images of the drug culture were back in full force. The reglamorization of the images of drug culture happened at the same time that the culture turned its attention away from the drug issue."

Some of the commercials chide parents for not taking the time to talk about drugs with their kids. A recent Partnership survey found that baby boomer parents, certainly knowledgeable about drugs from their own youth, are often strangely ignorant about the drug behavior of their own kids. In the survey, 21% of parents said it was possible that their kids might have used marijuana, while 44% of the kids said they had. Kids were also finding out about drugs at an earlier age, with the survey revealing that

90% of kids between the ages of 9 and 12 were aware of marijuana. Of that age group, the number of kids who had tried marijuana was 571,000 in 1997, up from 334,000 in 1993. To urge parents to step in and curb this problem, one ad features a dad who resorts to rapping as a way to communicate the dangers of pot use to his son. "The wacky weed it is bad, of this I know, believe your dad," he sings rather awkwardly, with boom box accompaniment from his wife. The message is that any way you talk to your kids about pot is a good way.

The Partnership's effort isn't the first time government and private groups have joined forces in the fight against marijuana. In the 1930s, for instance, the Federal Bureau of Narcotics enlisted the aid of women's groups and the National Congress of Parents and Teachers to speak out on the evils of marijuana.

Even after the Centers for Disease Control concluded that hundreds of American marijuana smokers were inhaling doses of paraquat that would produce lung damage, the U.S. Drug Enforcement Agency expanded the paraquat program for use in America.

Former U.S. Attorney General Ramsey Clark speaks out in favor of legalizing marijuana at a NORML conference held in November of 1998.

Policing the Pot Front

Enforcement of marijuana laws got off to a slow start. Cops had no idea what they were looking for when they were sent into the field to uproot marijuana plants. In 1936, law enforcement officials exhibited potted marijuana plants in Brooklyn precincts so that cops would be able to identify the offending growth when they saw it on their beats. Captain Joseph Mooney, head of the police narcotics division, announced in

July that he wanted to uproot every trace of the "loco weed" before it produced new seed by summer's end. The marijuana display paid off quickly. A few days later, two patrolmen spotted a marijuana crop spread over four lots in the borough's Bath Beach section.

Policing marijuana laws has become increasingly sophisticated, well-funded, and vigilant. Canadian police use Hyper Spectral Sensors to search for pot patches from the air. The sophisticated sensors were previously used by NASA to study interstellar gases, and are capable of spotting even the tiniest patch from

During the paraquat scare of the mid-'70s and early '80s, labs offering testing began springing up. Paranoid pot heads sent their stash to such companies as Pharm-Chem to be tested for paraquat.

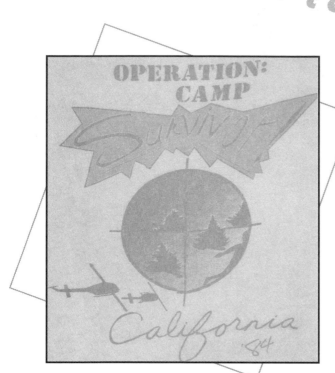

OPERATION:
CAMP
Survivor
California '84

"Dude, remember the choppers in '84?!"

American marijuana smokers were inhaling doses of paraquat that would produce lung damage, the U.S. Drug Enforcement Agency expanded the paraquat program for use in America.

The quest of Brooklyn police Captain Joseph Mooney to wipe out all of the marijuana in his district in 1936 is a goal often set on a much grander scale by state and federal drug police forces. Major efforts have been mobilized to eradicate it, but the weed keeps bouncing back, usually stronger than ever. Some of the major drives to wipe out marijuana have had the unintended consequence of doing just the opposite.

helicopters and airplanes. Some anti-marijuana campaigns take on the characteristics of military operations. The spraying of the herbicide paraquat, first used on Mexican marijuana crops in 1975, is reminiscent of Vietnam-style chemical warfare. The program was briefly suspended by Congress when reports surfaced that marijuana being sold and smoked in the United States contained dangerous traces of the toxic paraquat. After controversial studies on the dangers to public health of paraquat spraying, Congress lifted its ban in 1981. Two years later, even after the Centers for Disease Control concluded that hundreds of

Federal officials found out very early how anti-marijuana efforts might backfire. During the 1930s, criminals took advantage of the prevailing hype against marijuana by using it as a defense. After being caught committing a crime, they merely pleaded guilty—to being a marijuana smoker. That might get them off the hook by reason of insanity. Defense lawyers called federal narcotics agents to testify on behalf of their clients, and the agents were obliged to tell the jury that marijuana could indeed make people insane enough to commit horrible crimes against their will.

In 1969, a major federal anti-drug effort known as "Operation Intercept" was designed to block the supply of illegal drugs entering the U.S. from Mexico. Reports indicate that the effort severely cut the supply of inexpensive Mexican weed, causing a dramatic rise in street prices. In San Francisco, the cost for a lid of grass doubled from $7 to $15. Further up the supply line, dealers and big-volume buyers were spending $120 for a pound in Los Angeles, up from $90. The market responded to the crisis, however, as any free economy system would. Dealers began turning to other suppliers, tapping into more exotic marijuana strains from Columbia, Thailand, and Jamaica. Rather than wean people off pot, "Operation Intercept" only succeeded in introducing Americans to a higher-quality herb, while conditioning them to pay more for that extra kick. The government's anti-marijuana campaign instead created a generation of marijuana gourmets.

Another high-quality marijuana product that surged in popularity during the shortage of Mexican grass was hash. The U.S. Bureau of Customs had seized very little hash prior to 1966. That figure jumped by the end of the decade. Almost 200 pounds were seized at the border in 1968, and a whopping 623 pounds the following year.

Two decades later, another anti-marijuana campaign had the effect of enhancing America's marijuana marketplace. Federal agents launched "Operation Stop Crop" in 1988, designed by U.S. Attorney General Edwin Meese, to wipe out America's booming homegrown crop. The massive military-style eradication effort only made American growers more determined and creative. Growing moved indoors with a sophisticated array of hydroponic equipment, producing some of the best-quality marijuana that American smokers had ever experienced. Published reports estimated that the national marijuana yield actually increased during "Operation Stop Crop."

Still, by 1990, the volume of uprooted plants increased measurably, and remains high today. In 1994, the DEA destroyed 509 million plants, and seized more than $56 million in assets related to growing operations. That was up from the 1991 totals of 241 million plants destroyed and more than $40 million in assets seized. Federal agents now seize plants in every state, ranging in 1997 from a low of 65 in Wyoming to a high of 130 million in South Dakota.

Busted

Robert Mitchum and Lila Leeds leave court during their 1948 marijuana possession trial.

A pharmacy worker in Amherst, Massachusetts, recently looked over snapshots he had just developed for a customer. His attention was drawn to the customer's choice of a backdrop for his family portraits. The worker noticed five towering pot plants in the pictures. He promptly notified police, who arrested the man.

Most pot dealers, growers, and users make more of an effort to conceal their illegal activity. And yet thousands have been caught. In 1992, more than 340,000 people were arrested for marijuana violations, most for simple possession. By 1995, the figure was close to six hundred thousand, more than double the number of Americans busted in 1972. The following year marijuana arrests jumped to 642,000. In the past 25 years, more than 10 million Americans have been arrested on pot charges, according to the National Organization for the Reform of Marijuana Laws. The group estimates that as many as 17% of all federal prisoners are in jail on marijuana offenses.

Most people don't notice a pot arrest unless it involves someone they know personally—or if it's a celebrity. One of the earliest sensational pot busts involved Hollywood's celebrated bad boy Robert Mitchum. The noir star was nabbed in a Hollywood dope raid on August 31, 1948, caught red-handed with some reefer. Some outraged Americans called for a ban of his films. But after Mitchum served 60 days in jail, the public was more enamored of him than ever. His box-office appeal actually grew after he was exposed as a reefer head. Working as a brick-maker during his prison term, Mitchum was also a hit with fellow prisoners at the Wayside Honor Farm in Castaic, California. They voted him "Mr. Cement Block."

Mitchum is hardly the only famous inhaler charged with marijuana crimes. Through the years the lineup of celebrities busted for pot includes sports stars such as basketball's Chris Webber, Robert Parrish, and Allen Iverson, and tennis star Jennifer Capriati. Olympic snowboarder Ross Rebagliati was almost stripped of his gold medal after testing positive for pot at the Nagano Winter Games. Musicians snared under suspicion of pot smoking include Beatles John Lennon and Paul McCartney, jazz great Louis Armstrong, soul king James Brown, and rapper Queen Latifah.

Tommy Rettig, who played Lassie's boy-master Jeff Miller of the famous television series, served jail time in the 1970s for growing marijuana. More recently, Bob Denver, known to millions of television fans as Gilligan, was arrested after allegedly receiving more than an ounce of pot by mail. Imagining Gilligan as a closet toker gives a whole new meaning to his nickname, "Little Buddy," and may also explain why the castaways never made it off the island.

Pot and Taxes

While marijuana was first prohibited in America by a tax law, subsequent bans have made it more of a criminal issue than one of tax violation. Yet tax law continues to affect marijuana use in America. When an unnamed pilot crashed and died in Florida on a drug run, the IRS ruled that the street value of the pot stashed on the plane was part of his estate. That ruling came even though federal agents seized the marijuana crop. It added a $1.5 million tax bill to the pilot's heirs.

Stamps of approval.

In another ruling, the IRS determined that the money spent to buy pot for medical purposes is not deductible. You can look it up. The ruling is in the agency's code book.

One of the strangest tax consequences of marijuana use occurred in Arizona, where zealous anti-pot legislators passed a punitive bill that unwittingly legalized marijuana use. The lawmakers passed a bill requiring marijuana dealers to purchase tax stamps and licenses. The legislators knew that dealers would be reluctant to sign up for obvious reasons, so those that were caught by police would have the crime of tax evasion added to their charges.

The plan went awry when dealers quietly purchased the stamps by mail. Government officials were prevented by the law from disclosing the names of license buyers. In 1995, marijuana activists from Arizona turned the tax law into a political issue, claiming that it sanctioned the selling of marijuana. The courts initially agreed. When police arrested Peter Wilson, chairman of the state's National Organization for the Reform of Marijuana Laws (NORML) chapter, on marijuana possession charges, a judge ruled that because he was properly licensed by the state, prosecution amounted to "double jeopardy." The charges were dismissed.

After the ruling, other activists stepped forward to buy licenses, including hemp activist Richard Davis. A former marijuana grower in California's famed Emerald Triangle during the 1980s, Davis ran for

Activist Richard Davis and his traveling hemp museum.

Congress in 1986 on a platform of legalizing marijuana for personal use. The bid for office, while unsuccessful, turned him into a public speaker. He opened what he called a traveling hemp museum—a truck packed with pro-hemp literature and artifacts. He travels the country, setting up his portable museum displays at state capitol buildings and college campuses, attracting the media and informing the public.

When he found out about Arizona's law, Davis saw a chance for some positive media coverage. He incorporated a hemp business and held a press conference on the Arizona capital steps, announcing that he was going in to buy his marijuana license. Then he set himself up on the Arizona State University campus, dispensing pro-hemp literature by day and dealing gram bags of green buds by night from a nearby parking lot. He informed incredulous customers that it was perfectly legal because he was a state-licensed dealer. Davis included a small pamphlet describing the virtues of hemp in each gram baggie, and also put in a small piece of hemp cloth. "There'd be 50 people lined up every night," he remembers. "I'd sell out and have to run home and get some more bud. It was crazy because no one was bothering us."

Growing more bold, Davis set up amid the Super Bowl hoopla of 1996 and began telling perplexed sports journalists how he was going to sell marijuana during the championship game. He offered special $20 bags of "SupHerb-Bowl" buds to commemorate the event. With so many reporters in town chasing any kind of story, Davis got dozens of interviews. Reporters began calling the local district attorney's office, asking if they were going to prosecute. On the day of the Super Bowl, an undercover agent bought three grams of pot from Davis, and he was arrested.

Unfortunately for Davis, the courts were now turning against marijuana activists.

An unusual Super Bowl package.

Davis, and later NORML's Wilson, were no longer able to mention the state's tax law as part of their defense. When Wilson was retried on 10 felony marijuana charges in June 1998, police inadvertently almost allowed the tax stamps as evidence. When they presented one of Wilson's marijuana bags in court, Wilson's attorney demanded that it be shown to the jury, since it still had the state's tax stamp attached to it. Not wanting the jury to see it, the judge sent them from the courtroom and ordered the stamps removed. Wilson was convicted on 9 of 10 charges and sentenced to 4 months in jail and 5 years of supervised probation. Davis was also convicted on 3 felony counts and sentenced to 5 years of probation, 720 hours of community service and fined $3,000. Meanwhile, Arizona closed the marijuana tax loophole by repealing the law in 1997.

The Tell-Tale Smell

One factor aiding police detection of marijuana is the plant's identifiable pungent aroma. It's a smell that penetrates even the most diligent packaging efforts and causes the undoing of many pot dealers. In Washington, D.C., a dealer stashed his supply in what he thought was a safe spot—a quiet home in the affluent Chevy Chase neighborhood. His plans went awry when concerned neighbors, detecting an unusual smell, asked the gas company to check on the home, believing they were doing a neighborly deed. The gas company worker smelled something too, but said it wasn't gas. Eventually, the local police followed their noses to a stash of 151 pounds of marijuana with a street value of half-a-million dollars.

The give-away smell can only crash the party for pot tokers. Denizens of early "tea pads" caught on quickly, burning incense to cover up the aroma of their smoke. Police were savvy too. Training films as early as the 1950s point out that evidence of incense burning is de facto proof of marijuana use.

The marijuana bouquet gave away Francois Blanchette, who toked up while savoring a peaceful afternoon of carefree drawing on the University of Saskatchewan campus. Before he set up his easel, he smoked a joint to put him in a creative mood. He didn't know that his pleasure puffs were lifted by spring zephyrs to the nostrils of police officers taking a training course in a nearby classroom. Blanchette was arrested and charged with possession.

NORML Founder Keith Stroup speaks on behalf of his organization, which was founded in 1970.

The Legal Pipe Dream

A recreational toker's fantasy of a world where marijuana is legal came achingly close during the liberal 1970s. At the forefront of that battle was Keith Stroup, an attorney who founded a marijuana lobbying group that would become synonymous with the fight to legalize marijuana—the National Organization for the Reform of Marijuana Laws (NORML). After a 30-year effort to win legalization, NORML is no closer to that goal today than when it first started. "The effect of 15 to 20 years of the 'War on Drugs' has left its

impact. People are terrified to be honest about marijuana out of fear that they will be held up to ridicule by the community, or hurt if they run for public office," Stroup admits.

That's hampered the group from tapping into its built-in constituency of millions of marijuana smokers. The group has ten thousand members. "We have to demonstrate that times have changed, and that those who are willing to stand up and speak the truth about marijuana won't have their lives destroyed. It's a process. It will take some time," Stroup vows.

> "The effect of 15 to 20 years of the 'War on Drugs' has left its impact. People are terrified to be honest about marijuana out of fear that they will be held up to ridicule by the community, or hurt if they run for public office," Keith Stroup admits.

Marijuana activist Chris Conrad worries that the DEA's enforcement of drug forfeiture laws is one of the most effective weapons against pot.

effective weapons used against pot is the DEA's aggressive enforcement of drug forfeiture laws. Since the 1980s, the DEA has confiscated property from scores of suspected drug users and dealers, and reports of excessive enforcement abound.

Congressman Henry Hyde, working toward reform of these laws, says that 80% of all forfeitured property belongs to owners who are never charged with a crime. The federal agency keeps the property because the burden of proof for these seizures is far less than in proving the crime of drug use or dealing. The DEA says that it confiscated more than $645 million in property under the law in 1995. Conrad says that this issue had made marijuana users extremely fearful of speaking up. "Now there is way too much risk. Once they introduced property forfeiture, that changed the nature of the game," he points out.

Marijuana activist and author Chris Conrad believes that one of the most

> **"When the American public is concerned about the welfare of their kids, naturally they respond in a more conservative manner,"** Stroup observes.

Some groups are pushing for a more reasoned debate on drug laws. One of the more prominent voices in this category is a coalition of scientists and prominent Americans funded by billionaire philanthropist George Soros. The group believes in a drug policy based on "harm reduction," with less emphasis on criminal prosecution. Add to this mix some conservative thinkers, such as William F. Buckley, who have promoted the idea that drug use should be legalized.

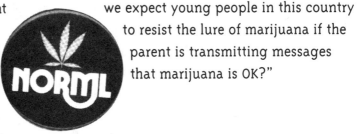

That battle is a tough one, Stroup admits. Another effective weapon against legalized marijuana, he concedes, is linking it to problems with American youth. "When the American public is concerned about the welfare of their kids, naturally they respond in a more conservative manner," Stroup

observes. Even so, public health officials worry that parents who once inhaled in their youth are reluctant to express deep worries about marijuana to their children. That could prove critical as teens continue to turn to marijuana. A recent government study shows that marijuana continues to be the drug of choice for American teens, with almost 10% of all 12- to 17-year-olds having tried it. First-time users are estimated at 2.54 million, up from 2.41 million in 1995. Health and Human Service Secretary Donna Shalala blamed parents for the increase, complaining, "How can we expect young people in this country to resist the lure of marijuana if the parent is transmitting messages that marijuana is OK?"

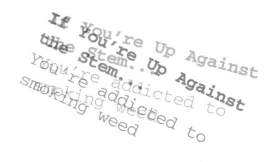

If You're Up Against the Stem...You're addicted to smoking weed

(Right) Making a case for a NORML society.

WHAT THEY SAY IS TRUE, MANY PEOPLE WHO SMOKE MARIJUANA —— MOVE ON TO HARDER THINGS. —— GRADUATE SCHOOL, FOR EXAMPLE.

http://www.norml.org

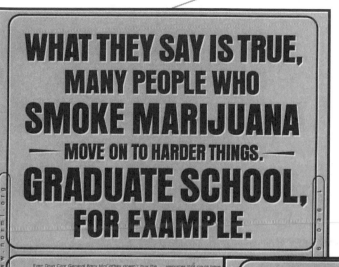

Even Drug Czar General Barry McCaffrey doesn't buy the argument that marijuana is a "gateway drug" that "leads to harder things." In a speech to the National Press Club, General McCaffrey stated that only a tiny percentage of the 90 million Americans who experiment with illegal drugs become addicts. He also said that the "overwhelming majority" of Americans who try illegal drugs simply "walk away and say it's not for me."

The Drug Czar was acknowledging what we at the National Organization for the Reform of Marijuana Laws, NORML, already knew. The vast majority of people who have smoked pot (i.e., Bill Clinton, Newt Gingrich, Al Gore) do not move on to harder drugs or run into drug related problems later in life. So why does our government spend $7 billion a year to arrest and jail people for this relatively harmless activity?

Like Alcohol Prohibition of the 1930's, Marijuana Prohibition is a failure. It has ruined productive lives, wasted criminal justice

resources that could have [been]
clogged up court and pr[...]
arrest[...]
who [...]
legitim[...]
of $25[...]
count[...]
1001 [...]
Wash[...]
a bi-m[...]
Suppo[...]
a min[...]
on a[...]
your s[...]

decrim[...]
regula[...]
and [...]
lower than here in the Un[...]
can always learn some[...]
without going to gradu[...]

IF YOU DON'T CARE ABOUT THE PEOPLE SENT TO PRISON FOR SMOKING MARIJUANA, —— AT LEAST CONSIDER —— WHO GETS RELEASED TO MAKE ROOM FOR THEM.

http://www.norml.org

Every day, violent criminals are released early from over-crowded prisons to make room for marijuana offenders. In 1995, there were 580,000 marijuana arrests, the most ever: 86% for simple possession. Because of harsh mandatory minimum sentences for even small amounts of pot, more people are serving hard time than ever.

The government spends an estimated $7 billion a year in this war against marijuana smokers. In a nation with 10 million violent crimes a year, surely we can find better ways to allocate our criminal justice resources. It's time to stop acting as if law-abiding citizens who happen to smoke marijuana are part of America's crime problem.

As courtrooms and prisons bulge with non-violent marijuana offenders, a growing number of active federal judges have come out in support of marijuana decriminalization, a policy endorsed by many respected groups. These include President Nixon's 1972 Commission on Marijuana, the National Academy of Sciences, the

California Research Advisory Panel, The Economist and National Review magazines, and two of Britain's most esteemed medical journals. Today, decriminalization works in Holland, a nation with much lower crime and hard drug usage rates than the U.S.

If you agree that it makes no sense to arrest people for using a substance less harmful than alcohol or tobacco, join NORML. With a donation of $25 or more, you can help change our country's marijuana laws. Write us today at 1001 Connecticut Avenue NW, Suite 1010, Washington, DC 20036, and we'll send you our bi-monthly newsletter. Or call the NORML Support Line at 1-900-97-NORML. For $2.95 a minute, 18 years or older, you'll receive up-to-date information on marijuana penalties in your state, drug testing, and your legal rights.

Like Alcohol Prohibition of the 1930's, today's Marijuana Prohibition is a failure. With your help, we can end it once and for all.

NORML.

Unusual Gag Order

One of the more unusual tales in the annals of pot crimes is the saga that unfolded on the eve of the 1988 presidential election. From his jail cell in Memphis, Tennessee, convicted drug dealer Brett Kimberlin was set to go public with his claim that he had once sold pot to vice presidential candidate Dan Quayle in the 1970s. As a jailhouse press conference was being set up, Kimberlin was ordered back to his cell for a strip search. He was then whisked away to solitary confinement, where he stayed until after the election. When asked to comment on the allegations by Kimberlin, Quayle accused him of lying, summing up Kimberlin's credibility by observing, "Geez, I mean, he's in jail."

What If?

If public tolerance of marijuana translates into legal action, how would a legal marijuana society function? Stroup believes that the most serious problems involving marijuana use stem from its prohibition, which has fostered the growth of an underground market and its associated crimes. Supporters of legalization imagine marijuana being regulated much like alcohol and tobacco. Laws would allow for adult use and create a government-regulated market of sellers.

In the 1970s, John Kaplan, a former U.S. attorney and a Stanford University law professor, wrote a book arguing for the legalization of marijuana and also pleaded his case on the lecture circuit. He saw marijuana being regulated like liquor. To curtail binge smoking, he saw a system of ration coupons to limit use. He suggested that taxes collected from marijuana sales be diverted into drug education programs in schools.

The Dutch Experience

While American marijuana smokers can only dream, tokers in other parts of the world can live out the fantasy of legal pot

enough to twist up about seven or eight joints. Amsterdam has about 350 of these clubs. They're adorned with simple neon signs and recognized by the exotic aromas wafting from their front doors. Dutch residents are also allowed to grow about five plants a year for personal use. While the Dutch government believes that its relaxed policy is working, other Europeans countries have complained that it's causing more illegal drugs to be imported into their own countries. Because of pressures from these countries, the Netherlands increased the minimum age for smoking from 16 to 18, and cut back the maximum amount for purchase from 1 ounce to the current level of 5 grams.

smoking. The Dutch government has taken a relaxed stance with soft drugs since the early 1980s, allowing the growth of coffee shops and pot-head bars where marijuana is freely bought and smoked. As long as neighbors aren't disturbed, owners of these cannabis clubs can openly sell about five grams of high-quality marijuana to each customer,

> **The Dutch government has taken a relaxed stance with soft drugs since the early 1980s, allowing the growth of coffee shops and pot-head bars where marijuana is freely bought and smoked.**

A budding law practice in Vancouver, B.C.

A similar relaxed atmosphere blossomed in the scenic tourist destination of Vancouver, British Columbia. Police began looking away as an Amsterdam-style smoking shop opened for business. Marijuana activist Marc Emery opened Hemp BC in 1993, offering seeds, a grow shop, and the resources of a legal clinic. Emery then added a Cannabis Cafe in 1997, which offers smoking samples. Marijuana is purchased in the open, with deals struck as diners munch on the latest in hemp foods. The enterprise's financial success spawned similar ventures. Opposition mounted and police shifted to a new approach after city officials were embarrassed by the city's growing reputation as "Vansterdam." Police made several raids and vowed to shut the clubs down. The new owner of the Cannabis Cafe, Sister Icee, is determined to remain open. Vancouver Mayor Philip Owen predicted that Icee's store was "going to be toast." But Icee shot back, telling a reporter, "Marijuana is a plant. You can't prosecute people for smoking flowers."

Yes, they can, if those flowers are marijuana. Thousands of flower smokers have been sent to jail since the introduction of marijuana laws in the twentieth century. The end is nowhere in sight. These laws have turned marijuana from a plant into a drug menace. Growing a crop that America's forefathers once treasured sends present-day citizens to prison. Marijuana offenders crowd the nation's jails, while high-volume marijuana smugglers are eligible for a punishment normally reserved for murderers: death. This harsh level of condemnation reflects a coldly negative view of marijuana. After all these years, marijuana is still treated as the menace that Anslinger said it was.

Jefferson Airplane
A bridge off one roach
clip for the
off a joint end

marijuana in the workplace

"may I have another cup, please?"

train engineer J.C. O'Day embarked on a very strange journey in 1899. About to make a freight run through north-western Pennsylvania, O'Day stopped at a pharmacy to pick up something for his nagging cough. The clerk recommended "Piso's Cure for Consumption," a medicine containing a hemp extract used to treat respiratory ailments. Unfortunately for O'Day, the healthy dose he downed before heading to work that day triggered a case of cannabis indica poisoning.

After only seven miles of track, O'Day's attention lapsed into a hashish daze, undermining his ability to drive his train. "I had forgotten," O'Day later recalled, "that the responsibility for the safety of the engine and the train rested on my shoulders." Oops. He began having visions, imagining that his legs were as large as smokestacks, his arms capable of encircling a flour barrel. When O'Day rumbled through a scheduled stop without slowing down, his fireman yelled, "O'Day, what is the matter with you?"

There was plenty wrong. O'Day was now seeing "dogs as large as Durham bulls" running after the train, barking wildly. He envisioned flocks of sparrows as large as condors. Despite being severely intoxicated, O'Day managed to complete his run without a catastrophe, greatly relieved when the mind-bending effects of the drug finally faded.

A nineteenth-century study of hash smoking in India noted that it was a common practice for laborers to end their day with a pull on the ganja pipe.

Giving Workers a Lift

Marijuana literally helped workers get back on their feet during the depression. The Work Projects Administration (WPA) employed crews to search for illegal marijuana crops sprouting up around New York City during the 1930s. The crews took their work seriously. In 1935, the WPA's marijuana patrol uncovered more than 260 growing sites around the city. In a 2-month stretch, they hauled in an incredible 170 tons of marijuana plants, a figure that attests to the WPA crew's vigilance—and the relative popularity of the drug with New Yorkers.

O'Day's experience is an obvious example of why cannabis intoxication and work sometimes don't mix. Under different circumstances, however, workers under the influence of cannabis drugs have found the experience more than beneficial. For centuries, warriors have shored up their courage before battle with a dose of marijuana or hashish. Scores of artists have incorporated marijuana smoking into the creative process, most notably jazz vipers of the 1930s, who wouldn't dream of showing up at a gig without their beloved Mary Warner.

In more pedestrian vocations, marijuana has offered countless workers relief from job tedium. Today, after-work toking has become a long-standing tradition. Meanwhile, a nineteenth-century study of hash smoking in India noted that it was a common practice for laborers to end their day with a pull on the ganja pipe or a few gulps of hash-laden *bhang*. This habit, researchers explained, helped workers "cheerfully bear the strain and perhaps the monotony of the daily routine of life."

Feed Bag
Container that holds marijuana

Mellow Yellow
The baked inner
scrapings of a
banana peel, passed
off in the '60s
as producing the
same effects as a
marijuana high

odds with society and not willing to conform to the demands of the workplace, never mind society at large. That reputation hasn't changed much over time. A recent survey of thousands of municipal workers found that those who smoked marijuana were less likely to commit to an organization. The results of this study were highlighted by the National Institute for Drug Abuse in its publicity campaign on the dangers of marijuana use.

The Dreaded Drug Test

THE DEFINITIVE GUIDE TO GUARANTEED CLEANSING RESULTS

Detoxify

Research you can count on. Products you can trust.™

Intense public pressure has led employers to take stringent measures to ensure that marijuana smokers never get on their payroll. The advent of widespread workplace drug testing began with the "zero tolerance" mentality of the war on drugs in the 1980s. Before this, courts had ruled that mandatory drug testing went against the Constitution. But the war mentality of the anti-drug campaign paved the way for the suspension of constitutional rights.

Bad Employees?

The prevailing American attitude is that a pot-smoking employee is a bad employee. One of the earliest condemnations of pot was that it made people lazy—a stigma that persists today. An early sociological study characterized reefer smokers as prone to "extreme inertness." Inertness, of course, no matter how acute, is not the mark of a productive employee.

Marijuana smokers are not considered prime candidates for the corporate world—or the factory line, for that matter. In the 1960s they were "anti-establishment," at

> **Marijuana, especially among more frequent users, can be detected in a worker's urine for up to six weeks. Meanwhile, users of cocaine, LSD, or opiates test clean only two days after using.**

Courts were now willing to sacrifice certain personal freedoms for the cause of creating a drug-free society. So Americans by the millions began peeing into cups as part of their job application. Aside from the indignity of this procedure, urine testing is particularly galling for marijuana smokers. Marijuana, especially among more frequent users, can be detected in a worker's urine for up to six weeks. Meanwhile, users of cocaine, LSD, or opiates test clean only two days after using. Pro-marijuana activists have

pointed to this chemical reality as an example of the unfairness of current drug-testing methods. The ultimate injustice is when a one-time toker who puffs at a party weeks ago tests positive, while another worker who regularly binges on alcohol and cocaine tests drug-free merely by abstaining for a couple of days.

The fear and reality of a positive test for marijuana has had a profound effect upon the workplace. It's caused marijuana users to make some hard choices between a recreational drug and their long-range career plans. If the user chooses to stay with marijuana, many career moves are off limits. For instance, almost all Fortune 500 companies conduct drug testing. And how many teenagers sit poised with their first joint pinched between their fingers and agonize over whether that one toke will one day prevent them from seeking public office?

The U.S. Labor Department reports that 40% of all American workers have been tested for drugs by submitting urine samples. In some fields, such as transportation, sports, and civil service, almost every worker will be tested. Those in "safety-sensitive" areas may also face

random on-the-job testing, theoretically prohibiting them from any drug use, even at home while not working.

The techniques for scanning large population segments for drugs were initially developed for the United States military. During the early 1970s, the U.S. army tested troops to uncover heroin addicts in its ranks. Other branches of the military followed suit—the need for a drug-free military overriding any question of invasion of privacy. The National Institute on Drug Abuse played a lead role in developing reliable methods of urine sampling.

In 1986, President Ronald Reagan issued an executive order declaring that all federal agencies be drug-free. Congress continued this sobering trend among civil servants by expanding the drug-free order to all federal workers, including contractors. NIDA began certifying dozens of labs for drug-testing work, and soon urine samples were being collected from millions of U.S. workers.

A comprehensive report on workplace drug testing, published in 1994 by the National Academy of Sciences, indicated that marijuana could have played a role in transportation accidents involving truck-ers, Navy pilots, and commercial train engineers. The NAS study also cited a survey of U.S. postal workers that used drug-test results to reach conclusions about the value of those workers. The study concluded that those who tested positive for marijuana were absent more often than those who tested clean, but not as often as those who tested positive for cocaine. Overall, however, those who tested positive for drugs were judged to be only slightly less valuable as workers than those who tested clean.

With more than 97% of the population testing negative, and some companies spending as much as $20,000 to find just

How many teenagers sit poised with their first joint pinched between their fingers and agonize over whether that one toke will one day prevent them from seeking public office?

one positive test, the report did question the overall effectiveness of workplace drug testing by stating: "The data obtained in worker population studies, however, do not provide clear evidence of the deleterious effects of drugs other than alcohol on safety and other performance indicators."

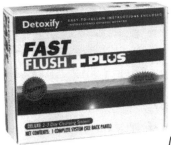

For when you really need that fast flush.

Beating the urine test is a booming market. NORML raises funds with a 900 help line for pot smokers looking to test negative for marijuana.

The Quest for Clean Urine

No one likes a cheater, of course. But with the odds stacked against marijuana smokers, some have resorted to bending the rules. Beating the urine test is a booming market. NORML raises funds with a 900 help line for pot smokers looking to test negative for marijuana. Meanwhile, an assortment of products available in head shops or through the Internet claim to rid the body of all traces of marijuana transgressions in a matter of a day or so.

Short of these products, advisors suggest increasing water intake before any urine exam. A large dose of B vitamins will darken urine that would otherwise appear too clear after water bingeing—a precaution against raising the suspicions of urine examiners. Other suggestions include taking diuretics, such as coffee and cranberry juice, or doctoring urine samples with Visine, bleach, salt, or cleaning solutions. Most testing labs are savvy to these techniques as well. They catch quite a few cheaters, often by checking for the obvious. One of the first things inspectors do is measure the temperature of a urine sample

Leaves hair silky and shiny! Works on dandruff too!

to make sure it hasn't been diluted with cooler toilet bowl water.

Even with readily available cheating methods, marijuana smokers do get caught. Marijuana is by far the most commonly detected illegal substance in the urine of prospective American employees. One of the largest drug-testing laboratories in the United States, SmithKline Beecham, reported that of all positive drug tests in 1997, 60% were for marijuana. Cocaine was a distant second at 16%. Overall, positive test results were found in about 5% of the 5 million drug tests, compared to 18% testing positive in 1987. While those who test positive for some drugs can claim charges of "false-positives," there are no longer accepted substances such as Advil that will lead to a false positive for marijuana. One strike, and you're out.

One of the first things inspectors do is measure the temperature of a urine sample to make sure it hasn't been diluted with cooler toilet bowl water.

Elbow

One pound of marijuana
One pound of marijuana

A Closer Inspection

While almost all drug testing in America is based on urine samples, future tests may result in more invasive techniques for gathering evidence of personal drug use. At the 1995 NIDA conference on marijuana, drug-testing experts offered a frightening vision of the more intrusive drug-detection methods that may become commonplace. Workers face testing of hair, saliva, blood, and even their sweat. Perspiration will one day be collected by a sweat patch applied to the body like a bandage to the skin. The patch will absorb bodily secretions, most likely sweat residue, which will be examined for evidence of drug use. Experts suggest that workers could wear this patch for up to several weeks.

While hair testing is rarely used, it is being promoted as a way to probe even

KLEAR

THE ULTIMATE PURIFIER IN 2 MICRO-TUBES

DIRECTIONS

1. KLEAR was perfected after thousands of hours of lab work. It is the smallest, and most potent purifier sold today. Add the contents of one tube of KLEAR to each urine sample. KLEAR dissolves almost instantly. Swirl your urine for a complete mix.

2. For best results on urine tests drink at least a quart of any liquid the day of the test. (Herbal teas are no better than water or coffee.) If possible take a 50 milligram B vitamin complex to turn your urine a nice golden color and impress the tester. Klear was carefully designed and fully tested for the basic urine screen given to all employees or job applicants.

3. KLEAR CLEARS ALL POSITIVES.

4. For large samples of more than 4 oz. use two tubes.

5. If kept away from moisture KLEAR remains potent up to 2 years. It is not sensitive to heat or cold.

6. Do not take internally. Klear is very powerful. Keep away from contact with skin or mucous membranes.

inevitable, marijuana advocates are searching for ways to stay ahead of new invasive testing methods. NORML, for example, points to recent research that touts shampoos that are effective at removing drug residues (the study endorses Head and Shoulders and Neutrogena over Pert and Prell).

further into an employee's past. Hair samples could yield evidence of drug use dating back several years. Those who believe they could beat the system with a crew cut should know that hair samples could be collected from any part of the body for testing. Gearing up for the

Gage in the Rough
Dirty weed

"Viva La Cucaracha!"

Pot Goes to War

For an intoxicant known for producing euphoria, marijuana would seem an unlikely candidate for military action. You'd expect to find marijuana at the peace conference, not on the battlefield. Many a marijuana philosopher has watched with dismay as world conflicts erupted, thinking, "Ah, if only they'd smoke some of this, they wouldn't want to fight." Glassy-eyed tokers, if challenged to battle, are usually inclined to respond, "Peace, brother!"

It's somewhat surprising, then, to realize that this laid-back plant is actually a battle-weary veteran. With varying success, marijuana and hashish have been used as an intoxicant by soldiers throughout history. Israeli soldiers on mop-up duty in the Sinai Peninsula after the Six Day War in 1967 discovered more than a ton of hash left behind by Egyptian soldiers. Some of Napoleon's troops returned from duty in the Middle East with a hash habit, causing concern among French commanders.

One band of fighters that relied heavily upon marijuana was headed by the flamboyant and brazen Mexican revolutionary fighter Pancho Villa. Military historians concede that this may have been history's first and only stoned army. Many fighters under Villa's command were Yaquis Indians who were known to use marijuana with regularity. Villa's theme song, which became one of the battle hymns of the Mexican Revolution, is the widely known "La Cucaracha" song. In Spanish, the words are, "La cucaracha, la cucaracha/Yo no puede caminar/Porque no tiene, porque no tiene/Marihuana que fumar." The

> **One band of fighters that relied heavily upon marijuana was headed by the flamboyant and brazen Mexican revolutionary fighter Pancho Villa. Military historians concede that this may have been history's first and only stoned army.**

translation is, "The cockroach, the cockroach/Can no longer walk/Because he hasn't, because he hasn't/Marijuana to smoke." For the record, historians credit Villa's troops with making a valiant effort in battle, sometimes fighting with a fanatic intensity, but other times wandering about in a confused state.

Before marijuana use among its own troops became a concern, the U.S. military tried to make it a problem for enemy forces. During World War II, the government's Office of Strategic Service was searching for a drug that would prompt captured enemy soldiers to give away military secrets. This search for a "speech-inducing" drug included tests with peyote, alcohol, barbiturates, and marijuana. The plant's intoxicating resin was distilled into a colorless and odorless liquid so it could be slipped into a drink served to enemy agents.

Years later, during Vietnam, American military leaders were worried that the

Vietnamese were turning that trick upon them. By the 1960s, American soldiers did have a pot problem, a trend that began with GIs stationed in Europe after World War II. A post-war study of American soldiers in West Germany discovered that half of the 36,000 troops assigned there had tried hash, and thousands of them were using it with enough frequency to be termed "hashaholics."

Keeping the peace with a buzz is one thing, but American GIs in Vietnam were reported to be toking up on high-grade marijuana while heading into battle. John Steinbeck IV, son of the great American novelist, stirred up the pot story when he returned from duty in Vietnam and claimed that three-quarters of his comrades were marijuana smokers. He came clean with this information after his own drug arrest in Washington, D.C. After this charge, *Newsweek* magazine sent correspondent John Donnelly into the field to find out how widespread the marijuana habit was among GIs. He reported back in November 1967 that marijuana was easy to come by, often sold disguised as filtered cigarettes, and of a potent variety known as Cambodia Red, a resinous strain grown in the Vietnamese highlands.

"One night in the central highlands," Donnelly recalled, "I watched ten GIs light up in a squad tent, while three North Vietnamese divisions lurked only a few miles away just across the Cambodian border." He also related stories of posh pot parties held in Saigon villas.

American commanders began taking action against pot smoking, presenting educational talks to soldiers and seeking the aid of the South Vietnamese govern-

4:20

Originally invented by a band called the Waldos whose members lit up at 4:20 in the afternoon, today, the tokers continue to follow in their tradition. Meanwhile, April 20 is fast becoming known as International Burn Burn day!

ment. Because only a small amount of marijuana was grown in Vietnam until the Americans showed up, the South Vietnamese showed little interest in punishing its own farmers for growing it. They saw it more as an American problem, which it was. During 1966, more than fifteen hundred servicemen in Vietnam were caught with it.

By 1970, Vietnam was producing more than 220,000 pounds of marijuana a year, and U.S. Army medical officers were estimating that 3 out of every 10 soldiers were smoking it up. Joints were readily available and cost between 5 and 15 cents. Marijuana smoking was definitely considered a negative factor in the American war effort. Senator Thomas Dodd of Connecticut was part of a congressional team looking into the problem, and he was quoted at the time as saying, "We have heard of marijuana being found on four out of five bodies of dead GIs, including officers, and of confused young men in combat turning to marijuana in sheer desperation."

By 1970, Vietnam was producing more than 220,000 pounds of marijuana a year, and U.S. Army medical officers were estimating that 3 out of every 10 soldiers were smoking it up.

Did marijuana cost Americans the war in Vietnam? It's a point worth considering. In Cheech and Chong's *Up in Smoke*, Chong infers as much when he and Cheech visit a deranged marijuana dealer in search of some smoke. When Chong learns that the dealer went crazy in Vietnam, he points out that Vietnamese pot was too strong for Americans and says, "That's why we lost the war, man."

Hay Head
Head: One who smokes marijuana
One who smokes marijuana

Pot and Politics

Marijuana has played a significant role in recent American political history. The "zero tolerance" test has been applied to many politicians, sometimes with devastating results. As an extreme case, consider the crushing blow suffered by Supreme Court nominee Douglas Ginsburg in 1987. A conservative circuit court judge, and a former professor at Harvard, Ginsburg was selected by Ronald Reagan after his original nominee, Robert Bork, went down in flames during a contentious confirmation process. Ginsburg's demise would be swift and sure, and all because of a few puffs of marijuana in social settings during the 1970s, more than a decade in his past.

Immediately after his nomination was announced, reports surfaced about Ginsburg's youthful marijuana experimentation, and the crisis was on. As leaders of the "Just Say No" campaign, the Reagan White House couldn't very well stand behind a man who had occasionally said,

"Sure, why not." Published reports began circulating about Ginsburg taking a few hits at parties, first as a law student and then as a professor. Considering the time period, it was an experience probably shared by millions. It didn't matter. Talk show jokes surfaced, mentioning how the revelation gave a whole new meaning to the term "high court." Reagan's conservative allies lobbied for Ginsburg's removal. Surprisingly, one of Ginsburg's few supporters was Attorney General Ed Meese, who found rare compassion for a law breaker, saying that Ginsburg's youthful puffing, so far in his past, shouldn't make him unfit for public service years later.

Head Gear
Any drug paraphernalia such as bongs, clips, or pipes

High Court

After only a few short hours of being blessed with the opportunity of a lifetime, to serve on the nation's highest court, Ginsburg was in seclusion, described by aides as feeling "let down." Within 36 hours of being nominated, he was forced to withdraw his name from consideration. He admitted to smoking pot on a few occasions, and offered a short but obviously bitter parting remark, "My views on the law . . . have been drowned out in the clamor."

For some reason, Ginsburg's sad saga moved others in the public spotlight to come clean. Marijuana mea culpas by politicians gearing up for a presidential run became the leading story. First, Democrat Jesse Jackson and Republican Jack Kemp said they had never used marijuana. They were followed by Arizona Governor Bruce Babbitt and Tennessee Senator Al Gore, who said they had. Another toker politician who came out of the closet at this time was Newt Gingrich, who added that he hadn't really liked it. Gore was methodical about his revelation, saying he had smoked as an undergraduate at Harvard, as an army correspondent, and as a reporter in Nashville. Gore likened it to drinking "moonshine." Apparently, the public sided with these confessing tokers; their revelations didn't cost them their public jobs.

Gore was methodical about his revelation, saying he had smoked as an undergraduate at Harvard, as an army correspondent, and as a reporter in Nashville. Gore likened it to drinking "moonshine."

A Smuggler's Résumé

Very rarely does an admission of past drug use work in someone's favor, but it did for convicted drug dealer Bruce Perlowin during the 1980s. Convicted as a marijuana smuggler, Perlowin was paroled after nine years in jail. Needing a job, Perlowin took the unusual step of promoting himself based on his experiences as the manager of a major marijuana smuggling operation.

In a résumé he sent around to several companies, Perlowin touted his organizational skills, his obvious attention to detail, and his strong business sense. He said he was looking to work for a progressive company that wouldn't hold his drug past against him. He also asked for employers to give special consideration to the fact that he was a marijuana dealer, and not someone who dealt in harder drugs such as cocaine. He pointed out that he had never used drugs himself because they impaired his ability to stay on top of his job. The résumé caught the eye of one firm in Oakland, California, and Perlowin was hired by Rainforest Products to be its national sales manager.

The High World of Sports

Aside from the politician, the person most likely to be scrutinized for drug use is the athlete. Considering that anti-marijuana forces have pointed to studies showing that marijuana use impairs motor skills, that athletes from a variety of sports have been unmasked as pot enthusiasts? Should we be surprised? It's been proven to be the recreational drug of choice for competitors ranging from surfers to NBA superstars.

Anthony Gobert, a top motorcycle racer, was forced to admit that he had a few celebratory puffs after a strong performance at a New Hampshire track. The Australian rider, nicknamed "Wild Child" for sporting varying hair dyes ranging from pink to fuchsia, was apologetic to his fans after the positive test, saying, "I would never do it before or during a race . . . I was wrong, just plain wrong." He was suspended for a month. The penalty for two Arena Football League players was more severe. When the Tampa Bay Storm team members tested positive for pot, they were suspended by the league for a year.

While many politicians can deftly deflect allegations of prior or current drug use with cleverly spun denials, the athlete has much less wiggle room. Competitors in most sports, from high school to the Olympics, face mandatory drug testing. College athletes began being tested on a large scale in the mid-1980s, even though an NCAA study found that drug use among athletes was mostly social and experimental. The survey of more than two thousand college athletes found alcohol to be the most prevalent drug used, with marijuana and hash a distant second and third. Still, testing was in, and soon the NCAA and the professional leagues followed suit.

In baseball, for example, after some highly publicized player arrests for cocaine violations, Commissioner Peter Ueberroth pushed for testing, saying in 1985 that, "A cloud hangs over baseball. It's a cloud

79

called drugs." One year later, the Baltimore Orioles became the first team to institute drug testing of its players. That same year, the New England Patriots, after suffering a blowout loss in the Super Bowl, imposed drug testing on its players.

While many elite athletes have become adept at masking use of sophisticated performance-enhancing drugs, concealing marijuana use is a major challenge. Like their unfortunate tokers in the world of politics, athletes have been haunted by positive marijuana tests, earning suspensions and losing status with coaches and fans.

In baseball, flamboyant pitcher Bill "Spaceman" Lee admitted that he smoked marijuana regularly, which may not have surprised many followers of the game. Lee was known for making unusual comments and tweaking the game's management powers, including his manager Don Zimmer, referred to by Lee as "the gerbil." When Zimmer demanded an apology, Lee

> **While pitching for the Expos, Bill "Spaceman" Lee told reporters that he used to sprinkle marijuana on his pancakes for breakfast every morning.**

obliged—by apologizing to gerbils everywhere. While pitching for the Expos, Lee told reporters that he used to sprinkle marijuana on his pancakes for breakfast every morning. Commissioner Bowie Kuhn wasn't amused and Lee was fined $250 in 1979.

The consequences were more severe for Orlando Cepeda, a former star who played for 17 seasons and was one of the game's most feared sluggers. However, after a year out of

baseball in 1975, he was arrested for marijuana smuggling in Puerto Rico, convicted, and sentenced to five years. When he got out after serving 10 months of his sentence, baseball didn't want him anymore. Cepeda believes that his drug conviction hampered his nomination to baseball's Hall of Fame.

In football, a record-breaking college wide receiver who tested positive for marijuana use as a sophomore was downgraded for the 1998 professional draft. While Randy Moss of Marshall University finished fifth in the Heisman voting after setting single-season NCAA records for touchdowns and receptions, he was bypassed by 19 teams before being selected by the Minnesota Vikings. Officials at some teams were vocal about raising the "character" issue in keeping him off their draft lists. Moss reacted to the snub by putting himself through a stringent preseason workout program, proclaiming, "I feel as the season goes on, somebody will have to pay." Picking up the tab once the season began were NFL cornerbacks, as Moss snared a string of touchdown passes and emerged as one of the top wide receivers in the league.

The marijuana issue slowed down Phil Jackson's coaching career. The former

Snowboarding added a whole new flavor to the Winter Games.

player with a decidedly counterculture bent admitted to smoking marijuana in a biography, and because of that, he was initially passed over for NBA coaching positions. When he finally overcame that stigma, Jackson became one of the game's greatest coaches, guiding the Chicago Bulls to several world championships.

One Rippin' Dude

Prior pot use almost proved disastrous for one Olympic athlete at the Nagano Winter Games in 1998. When the International Olympic Committee invited snowboarders to compete in its hallowed competition, it should have been prepared

81

to embrace all that went with it—including the youthful, colorful character of the typical snowboarder. It was hardly shocking when one of them tested positive for marijuana. What was surprising, however, was that the participant testing positive was Canadian Ross Rebagliati, the gold medal winner in snowboarding's giant slalom. Before Rebagliati's friends could say, "Way to go, dude!" the IOC stripped away his medal. Just as quickly, the Court of Arbitration for Sport reversed the IOC's decision, ruling that there was no clear provision in the rule book for marijuana testing at the Olympics.

Public reaction was mostly polite amusement. For Rebagliati, the whole affair was a nightmare. He endured five hours of interrogation from Japanese police, who searched his room looking for signs of any leftover buds. Rebagliati claimed he got marijuana in his system through a contact high at a party, making him an unfortunate victim of secondhand pot smoke. "I may have to wear a gas mask from now on," he joked with reporters. He didn't mention giving up his friends. After the Games, he asked hockey star Wayne Gretzky to put in a good word for him at the powerful Canadian sports agency IMG; the Great One obliged,

helping the young snowboarder get signed to endorsement contracts, including a deal with Roots, a Canadian clothing company.

Three months after the Olympics, the IOC announced that it was adding marijuana and other "social drugs" to its list of banned substances, even though they were not considered performance-enhancing drugs. The IOC's Dick Pound was quoted as saying, "The IOC had decided in the case of social drugs that we should take a stand, and Olympic athletes should be put to a somewhat higher

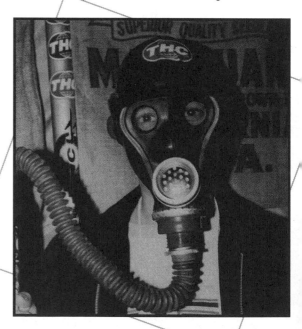

Future party attire for athletes?

standard than society in general." This so-called "Rebagliati Rule" became an issue for organizers of other athletic events, with some following the lead of the IOC and others insisting that marijuana use was of no consequence to sports. The Australian Cricket Board, for example, decided to impose random drug testing for its athletes, but decided not to include marijuana on its list of banned substances. The medical advisor of the Commonwealth Games of 1998 also reached the same conclusion.

Well before mandatory drug testing, marijuana contributed to the downfall of another boarder—world champion surfer Jeff Hakman. An international surfing star during the 1960s and 1970s, Hakman tells the darker side of his sunny success in the water in a biography by Phil Jarratt called *Mr. Sunset*. Hakman hollowed out surfboards and smuggled Lebanese hash into California from Mexico. At the time,

Hakman was endorsing surfboards made by Plastic Fantastic of Huntington Beach, California. The boards were promoted as being so good that they would "boggle your brain." The inside joke was that many of these boards contained high-potency hash that really would cook your mind.

Hakman proved to be a bungling smuggler, though, eventually getting caught trying to ship high-grade Thai marijuana to his home in Hawaii from an overseas U.S. army base. He was able to escape prison on a technicality. As Hakman relates, hash and marijuana were just some of the drugs used by surfers during this period to enhance their sport.

THC in the NBA

One pro sport where marijuana use appears to be the most prevalent is basketball. A *New York Times* report in 1997 suggested that as many as 70% of the players in the NBA smoke marijuana and drink excessively. The article quoted former player Richard Dumas, himself banned for substance abuse, as saying, "If they tested for pot, there would be no league."

That theory will be put to the test. As a part of the new bargaining agreement, negotiated during the lockout of 1998-1999, the league won the right to test players for marijuana, falling in line with America's baseball, football, and hockey leagues. The league was taking action to counteract marijuana arrests that had snared several of the NBA's rising young talent, including Marcus Camby, Allen Iverson, Isaiah Rider, and Chris Webber. Billy Hunter, director of the player's association, was using the marijuana testing issue as leverage during negotiations on a new contract, agreeing to it if the league agreed to some of the players' demands. Hunter observed, "If there is a marijuana problem, it's one reflective of society."

What was happening in the NBA was happening on a larger scale at workplaces across America, and elsewhere in the world where drug testing is the norm. There was a stated goal for a drug-free workplace, and yet there were millions of pot-smoking workers, from blue collars all the way up to a Supreme Court justice and a two-term president. The battle line was drawn, then, between the drive for a workplace free of marijuana, and one manned by workers in a society where pot smoke drifted through the air.

A *New York Times* report in 1997 suggested that as many as 70% of the players in the NBA smoke marijuana and drink excessively. The article quoted former player Richard Dumas, himself banned for substance abuse, as saying, "If they tested for pot, there would be no league."

marijuana as medicine

"smoke two joints and call me in the morning"

marijuana as a medicine has a curiously long history that has been mostly forgotten.

Medicinal marijuana dates back thousands of years. It was first prescribed as far back as 2737 B.C. in China, and was recorded in Han Dynasty court documents as being used to treat rheumatism, fevers, gout, and to relieve pain during childbirth.

In Europe and North America, marijuana began to be recorded in medical guides during the sixteenth and seventeenth centuries. A British Dispensary guide in 1682 suggested that hemp seeds could be used to cure coughs and jaundice, but had the side effect of filling the patient's head with "vapors." A later medical guide recommended boiling hemp roots and applying the resulting potion to the skin to reduce inflammation and to dissolve joint deposits.

During the nineteenth century, hemp compounds and cannabis tinctures were suggested for a number of ailments, including gout, joint pain, nose bleeds, cholic, and to "allay the troublesome humours in the bowels."

There are reports that cannabis was used to treat diarrhea and dysentery during the Civil War, and was even applied as a pain reliever.

There are reports that cannabis was used to treat diarrhea and dysentery during the Civil War, and was even applied as a pain reliever. The U.S. Dispensary of 1854 listed hemp compounds as suggested remedies for a multitude of medical problems, including neuralgia, depression,

85

Shen Nung, ancient Chinese emperor, is the author of the oldest known pharmacopoeia, which included the use of marijuana as medicine.

nineteenth century, however, just as industrial hemp fell out of use, so did medical cannabis. There were several problems with marijuana as a medicine, some which linger today. The potency of cannabis preparations varied widely from pharmacy to pharmacy, making it difficult for doctors to control patient doses. What worked perfectly for one patient could send another into a frightening delirium. Cannabis is also not soluble in water so it can't be given by injection. Morphine can, however, and it is easier to control and faster-acting. Doctors could administer a shot of morphine and soon be on their way. If they prescribed cannabis, they'd have to stick around for an hour or more to see the results, and be ready to spring into action in case of a severe negative reaction.

hemorrhage, pain relief, and muscle spasms. It could also be helpful in inducing sleep, stimulating appetite, and even boosting the sex drive. These applications came with the warning that doses could cause intoxication, stupor, and hallucinations. Toward the end of the

These drawbacks didn't stop pharmaceutical companies, including the Squibb Company, from making several cannabis medications. But gradually cannabis disappeared from medicine cabinets across America, and formal prescriptions vanished completely after passage of the Marijuana Tax Act of 1937.

Three Fluid Ounces
Cold Treatment
Cough Syrup

ALCOHOL, 10 per cent
CANNABIS,
CHLOROFORM,
in each fluid ounce combined with
Lobelia, Balsam Tolu, Tartar Emet-
ic and Ammonium Chloride.

A reliable expectorant, giving
prompt relief of cough in Colds
and bronchitis It has a sooth-
ing effect upon the
mu   and
stimulates expectoration.

Directions: One or two teaspoon-
fuls every 2 or 3 hours, for adults.
Children over twelve, 1 2 teaspoon-
ful; over five, 10 to 20 drops; infants,
3 to 10 drops.

Distributed by
TANCRO DRUG CO.
NEW YORK

Complete Cold Treatment

Cannabis was a popular ingredient in many late
nineteenth/early twentieth century remedies.

℞ CANNAB.IND.

87

THCALIFORNIA INDICA

California voters have been medical marijuana friendly.

Widespread Debate

As the history of medical marijuana began to be widely publicized in the 1980s and 1990s, campaigns to make marijuana legal for medicinal purposes gained momentum while igniting widespread debate. Proponents were pushing for marijuana to be legalized for a variety of medical applications, including combating the nausea from chemotherapy treatments, the wasting-away syndrome in AIDS sufferers, and even the uncomfortable symptoms associated with PMS. A majority of states passed laws supporting the medical use of marijuana, but these proved to be largely ineffective. The federal government kept a

FIGHT AIDS

NOT MARIJUANA

tight seal on any plans for prescription marijuana. That prompted voters in Arizona and California to go a step further, passing propositions making medicinal marijuana legal. Arizona's bill was gutted by an outraged state legislature, but two years later, voters fought back and approved two initiatives that restored the original language. Also passing medical marijuana laws in 1998 were Alaska, Washington, Oregon, and Nevada.

Medical marijuana is clearly an issue that resonates with the public. An ABC television poll in 1997 found that 7 out of 10 Americans supported it, even though an overwhelming number of them were opposed to legalizing marijuana for recreational use. Former World Wrestling Federation star Jesse "The Body" Ventura took a maverick stand in favor of medical marijuana and scored an upset victory in the race for governor of Minnesota in 1998. More conventional support for the movement comes from the ACLU and the American Medical Association. While serving as U.S. Surgeon General, Joycelyn Elders voiced her belief that doctors had the right to prescribe marijuana as

Former World Wrestling Federation star Jesse "The Body" Ventura took a maverick stand in favor of medical marijuana and scored an upset victory in the race for governor of Minnesota in 1998.

substance. One Simi Valley, California, resident decided to go to local police and let them know he was growing a few plants for his own medical use to combat a variety of ailments, including skin cancer and diabetes. The police responded by arresting him and charging him with felony cultivation. Although a judge later dismissed the charge, when the police returned his stash, it was moldy and unusable.

In states with no legal provision for medical marijuana, the penalties for patients can be severe. Paraplegic Jim Montgomery was discovered by police in Oklahoma with two ounces of pot in his wheelchair pouch. He was using it to relieve muscle spasms. He was tried and convicted in 1992 on charges of intent to distribute and possession of paraphernalia. He was sentenced to life in prison plus 16 years. A judge reduced the jury sentence to 10 years. With these types of consequences, it's no wonder that most patients continue to use marijuana as they always have: secretly at home, with a wary eye on getting caught for choosing a medicine that happens to be illegal.

medicine. Many doctors agreed. A Harvard University survey of more than a thousand cancer specialists found that 44% had recommended marijuana to a patient, and almost half said they would prescribe it if it were legal. Similar results were recorded by the British Medical Association, which found that 74% of its members polled in 1997 were in favor of prescription marijuana.

Growing public support still hasn't brought medical marijuana into the open. Even with protective laws, some patients still get arrested on drug charges, while doctors are reluctant to prescribe an illegal

Club Med

"It makes you smarter. It touches the right brain and allows you to slow down, to smell the flowers," says Dennis Peron, seen here at the San Francisco Buyers' Club, the organization he formed.

One of the oldest clubs was in San Francisco, operated from 1992 to 1996 with the tacit approval of city authorities. It was formed by Dennis Peron, a colorful figure and outspoken marijuana proponent who considers all forms of marijuana use "medical." "It makes you smarter. It touches the right brain and allows you to slow down, to smell the flowers," Peron says of marijuana.

Getting medical marijuana initiatives passed has proven much easier than actually putting such laws into practice. A major obstacle has been how medicinal marijuana can be legally distributed to patients who have doctor's approval to use it. One method emerged in California with the development of so-called cannabis buyers' clubs. These clubs featured an unusual atmosphere and subculture that was a mix of hash house and medical clinic.

Peron's popular club, a concrete and glass structure on busy Market Street, pumped in Grateful Dead music and featured a Jerry Garcia elevator. There was a daily menu of pot specials that included a variety of baked goods and cannabis tinctures. Patients relaxed and dosed themselves in a comfortable lounge area outfitted with thrift-store couches and psychedelic art on the walls.

The club was dispensing pounds of marijuana weekly to more than a thousand patients, so it's not surprising that it attracted the attention of state and federal authorities. In 1996, just as Prop. 215 was gaining momentum, Peron's club was raided by California drug agents, who seized 150 pounds of pot and more than $60,000 in cash, and closed the club down. Lower profile clubs have since opened in San Francisco to fill the medical marijuana void. California Attorney General Dan Lungren, an outspoken critic of Prop. 215, accused Peron of allowing teens to buy pot and also having infants present in patient smoking rooms.

After passage of 215, drug agents raided another cannabis club in the Bay Area, seizing dozens of plants and growing equipment and effectively shutting it down. The agents said that the

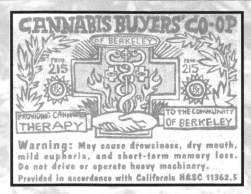

This Cannabis Buyers' Co-Op sticker is placed on the marijuana container given to buyers.

club was giving out too much pot to patients. Of the more than two dozen cannabis clubs that emerged after the passage of 215, fewer than 10 remained by the end of 1998. Even though Oakland offi- cials took special measures to keep the city's Cannabis Buyers' Cooperative open, it was ordered closed by a federal judge in October 1998. Oakland's City Council had voted to appoint members of the cannabis club as city officers in an attempt to shield them from prosecution. However, the judge ruled that, despite 215, the sale of marijuana was illegal under federal law.

In December 1998, Buyers' Cooperative won approval to reopen while an appeal is being heard—but only on the condition that no marijuana be involved

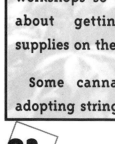

R̶ CBC
The Los Angeles Cannabis Buyers Club

serving
Patient Communities
throughout the
Greater Los Angeles Area

CALIFORNIANS FOR COMPASSIONATE USE

Would you like to work for a more compassionate society?

A coalition is forming to change the laws that prohibit the use of medical marijuana, to allowing its use and cultivation legally with a doctor's prescription. This coalition's only goal is to relieve suffering. It is open to all who share in that goal. Join us for a more just and compassionate society.

The group will collect 500,000 signatures, commencing approximately in August of 1995 for the November '96 ballot.

"The Compassionate Use Act of 1996"

"Join us in our quest for a more just and compassionate society."
– Dennis Peron

them. They hoped to shed the image of free-wheeling pot parties in favor of more sober-minded medical facilities. They worked closely with local police and drug agents to make sure there weren't problems.

In San Jose, Peter Baez, a colon cancer patient, worked with local police to develop an operation system that regulated how much marijuana could be on site and how much a patient could buy. The city also insisted that the cannabis center grow its own supply. When Baez worried about how he could pull this off, local police were kind enough to provide growing tips. Baez prefers to call the operation a "center" rather than a "club." It's all business here. Patients order from a menu board, and even pay with a credit card. The center, located in an office park, even has a city business license.

Another model operation is in West Hollywood, where Scott Imler, one of the co-authors of Prop. 215, heads a cannabis

in the operation. The Co-op was planning to open a hemp store and host how-to workshops so that patients could learn about getting medical marijuana supplies on their own.

Some cannabis clubs survived by adopting stringent rules and sticking by buyers' club serving almost one thousand patients. Most of them are AIDS sufferers, but others are being treated for cancer, glaucoma, chronic pain, and epilepsy. Imler himself began smoking marijuana to combat cluster headaches and seizures that developed after he suffered a head injury in a skiing accident. His relationship is so good with the local sheriff's office, that Imler believes if a raid were to happen, local authorities would politely tip him off.

Scott Imler, head of the Los Angeles Buyers' Club, takes marijuana for his own medical condition, which consists of cluster headaches and seizures from a skiing accident.

The West Hollywood center is located in an upstairs storefront on a busy street. There's an ordering bar and a living room where patients can take their dose of either smokeable marijuana or baked goods. To make it less of a party atmosphere, Imler has imposed a "no passing" rule on joints. "We felt an obligation to implement what we believed was the intent of the voters," Imler maintains.

Imler, however, has grown disillusioned with the whole medical marijuana movement. He watched with dismay as Peron and Lungren waged a high-profile media battle in San Francisco over the issue. Imler believes that Peron's "all marijuana use is medical" mantra has hurt the movement tremendously.

"Dan Lungren did everything possible to defeat this, and Dennis Peron did everything possible to exploit it. Basically, the patients were left in the middle," he notes sadly. "We've just given the opposition every reason to crush us and close the clubs down. People have been loose, abusive, and greedy, and it just turns my stomach." While Imler still believes that marijuana should be available as a legal medicine, he no longer believes that the cannabis club format is the way to go.

Dr. Lester Grinspoon is the author of the book *Marijuana Reconsidered*. A professor at the Harvard Medical School, Grinspoon is considered to be one of the foremost authorities on marijuana.

A Tough Pill to Swallow

Anti-drug forces developed a strategy of attack against the medical marijuana movement by insinuating that it was just a cleverly disguised attempt to make recreational pot legal. The federal government remains strongly opposed to medicinal marijuana, even though it's convened conferences designed to evaluate its worth. After California and Arizona passed medical marijuana laws in 1996, U.S. drug czar Barry McCaffrey and U.S. Attorney General Janet Reno threatened doctors who prescribed pot with having their licenses revoked. "We want to make it clear that

federal law still applies," Reno warned. That was all she needed to say. Marijuana wasn't a medicine in the government's mind. It was just another illegal drug that needed to be controlled.

The U.S. Office of National Drug Control Policy, while issuing a statement saying that its position is based on science rather than ideology, nonetheless can't hide its distaste for the medical marijuana movement. Talk of marijuana as medicine, the office stated, "sends a confusing message to our children concerning marijuana that could not have come at a worse time . . . The increase in marijuana use has been fueled by a measurable decrease in the proportion of young people who perceive marijuana to be a dangerous substance." Even while announcing that the government's National Academy of Science would launch an investigation into the issue, the drug policy office stated that it won't welcome results showing that marijuana is a useful medicine. The national drug office statement concluded, "Our nation's goal must be to reduce, not promote, the use of illicit drugs." So much for science over ideology.

The National Institutes of Health also went through the motions and convened a panel in 1997 to study the issue. Its conclusions were luke-warm in favor of more research. A summary stated that "there were varying degrees of enthusiasm to pursue smoked marijuana for several indications. This enthusiasm was tempered by the fact that for many of these disorders, effective treatments are already available . . . more and better studies would be needed."

That much is true, of course, but those studies may never get done because all marijuana research needs the approval of a government that is decidedly against medical marijuana. Researchers wishing to study the medicinal effects of marijuana have to pursue an elaborate and cumber-some application process that shuffles through several layers of government bureaucracy.

> **All marijuana research needs the approval of a government that is decidedly against medical marijuana. Researchers wishing to study the medicinal effects of marijuana have to pursue an elaborate and cumbersome application process that shuffles through several layers of government bureaucracy.**

Homegrown Medicine

Medicinal marijuana clearly faces an uphill battle. One of marijuana's obvious problems is that many patients aren't comfortable with the idea of smoking something illegal or, for that matter, taking a drug that will get them high. Physicians would like to prescribe it to their patients, but many are worried about the damaging effects of smoking on the lungs. This concern is critical with AIDS patients, who may further compromise an already damaged immune system by smoking marijuana. It's an issue that hasn't been adequately tested, even though thousands of AIDS patients are using pot to combat the wasting-away syndrome of the disease.

Bubble-Bubble
Water-cooled pipe

Judge, It's a Medicine—Really!

Like many of his peers during the 1960s, Robert Randall sailed through college on a "cloud of cannabis." He enjoyed smoking pot in groups or alone, drifting off into pleasurable waking dreams. What Randall didn't know then was that a few years later marijuana would become infinitely more significant to him than just an idle delight; it would literally save his sight.

After college, Randall moved to Washington, D.C., where one summer night he realized that he could no longer read with his right eye. All he could detect were a jumble of incoherent black shapes on white paper. The next day an ocular pathologist gave him the sad news: He had glaucoma. Within five years he could go blind.

Over the next several months, Randall pursued every glaucoma treatment offered by traditional medicine, from potent drops to pills. Not only were the medications ineffective, they caused devastating side effects, including crushing fatigue and heart palpitations. One night he smoked a marijuana cigarette and made a startling discovery: The tricolor halos he was used to seeing around lights suddenly disap-

In 1998, the NIH finally agreed to fund a $1 million study at the University of California at San Francisco that's designed to examine the effects of marijuana smoking on the immune system, and to test its interaction with antiviral drugs such as protease inhibitors. Under the direction of Donald Abrams, the study should give AIDS patients much-needed data on how effectively marijuana works for them as a medicine.

peared. What was happening? He remembered that when he had experienced mild vision problems in college, marijuana smoking had seemed to help. Could it be, he thought, that smoking pot was somehow easing his glaucoma symptoms? This was a crazy idea. Conventional wisdom, Randall knew, was that marijuana distorted your vision, not cleared it up. "I thought it was a little flaky to believe that all the modern pharmaceuticals were not working, but a plant that I enjoyed using was going to save my sight. It seemed a little delusional," Randall recalls.

The proof surfaced during his next doctor's visit. An examination confirmed that his eye pressure had dropped to safer levels. His sight was improving. If the trend continued, his long-term prognosis would dramatically improve. His doctor was dumbfounded. After much thought, Randall decided not to let him in on his secret. Would the doctor have ever believed him? He kept on smoking in private, and his condition continued to improve.

Randall might have continued this way but a police raid brought his private prescription medicine out in the open.

Charged with growing marijuana, Randall had no choice but to mount a criminal defense. When he told his lawyers that he was using pot to help his eyesight, they had a good laugh. Then Randall told them again: Yes, I'm really smoking pot to save my eyesight. They began to take him seriously.

Randall dug around for information. Imagine his surprise when he discovered that medical researchers were already aware that marijuana was useful in treating glaucoma, although no one had ever told him. Researchers at UCLA in 1971 were

Researchers at UCLA in 1971 were conducting a study for the Los Angeles Police Department designed to determine if pot smoking caused pupils to dilate... What the researchers found instead was that marijuana smoking lowered intraocular eye pressure — an effect extremely beneficial to glaucoma patients.

conducting a study for the Los Angeles Police Department designed to determine if pot smoking caused pupils to dilate. The police were hoping that if this were true, they could use this as evidence to search vehicles on the basis of marijuana intoxication. What the researchers found instead was that marijuana smoking lowered intraocular eye pressure—an effect extremely beneficial to glaucoma patients.

A sweet prescription: the government's tightly rolled joints dispensed in a tin.

To prepare for his criminal case, Randall underwent testing at UCLA and, later, Johns Hopkins. He was mounting a medical neces-

sity defense, a rarely used tactic that almost always fails. To prove his case, Randall would have to show that no other available medication was helpful. "With conventional treatment, I was right on schedule for going blind. It wasn't enough to say that I preferred marijuana. It had to be an absolute necessity, and that consequences would occur. In my case, it was blindness," Randall remembers. The two intensive tests he underwent proved his case. Only marijuana was useful in lowering his eye pressure. As a result, he was acquitted of the cultivation charges in 1976.

Not willing to stop there, Randall then sued the federal government to be included in its new compassionate-use drug program. He no longer wanted to buy his drug on the black market, or risk further criminal charges by growing his own. He won that case as well. As a result, Randall became the first American to be legally supplied with marijuana grown by the U.S. government. Every month he goes to a local pharmacy and picks up a silver cookie tin containing three hundred tightly rolled joints. Other patients followed

Glaucoma sufferer Elvy Musikka was the first woman to receive medical marijuana.

After suffering massive injuries from a motorcycle accident, Steve McWilliams began smoking marijuana to ease his pain. McWilliams was actively involved in the campaign to pass California's Proposition 215 to legalize the use of marijuana as medicine.

the U.S. Public Health Service (PHS) was swamped with compassionate-use applications for marijuana, with many coming from AIDS patients. James Mason, head of th PHS, declared that the growth of the program was giving the public the impression that the government condoned marijuana use, so the PHS revoked its approval of 28 applications, and canceled the program. Only the original 13 were allowed to continue. Since then, six have died and seven remain, including Randall.

Randall's lead and applied for the compassionate-use program, with 13 original people being approved. Among them was Elvy Musikka, a glaucoma patient and the first woman to receive medical marijuana from the government beginning in 1988. She's been an outspoken supporter of legalizing marijuana as medicine.

The application process for the compassionate-use program was time-consuming, so Randall's organization, the Alliance for Cannabis Therapeutics, developed a simple how-to kit that streamlined the process. The group's forms were so easy to use that by the early 1990s

Randall's trial and lawsuit against the federal government were landmark events that changed the history of medical marijuana in America. They forced the public to make the same startling realization that Randall concluded after his halo-reducing puffs that summer night in 1972: pot could indeed be a medicine. It's an idea that requires people to shift their views about medicine, and marijuana. Most medicine comes from a pharmacy prescription bottle, not rolled in a joint. And medicine certainly isn't something you smoke. As a plant that patients can easily grow at home, marijuana bypasses the pharmaceutical industry, making it a threat to major drug companies.

Uncle Sam's Pot Farm

William Faulkner

Just where are these compassionate-use patients getting their legal marijuana? Smack in Oxford, Mississippi, a town known for its literary giants William Faulkner, Eudora Welty, and John Grisham. The country's only legal pot farm is located on the University of Mississippi campus. It began in 1968 when a researcher was awarded a federal grant to study marijuana at a time when recreational use was growing in popularity. With a crop already started, the government has maintained the program ever since, using it to supply marijuana for research programs around the country.

On the farm's closely guarded seven acres, workers grow enough pot to produce more than thirty thousand joints a year. The U.S. Drug Enforcement Agency supplies the seeds. Harvesting is done by the combined efforts of 14 permanent workers and seasonally hired university students, who undergo stringent security checks. The plants are then cured in a barn once used to dry tobacco. Then barrels of the harvest are shipped by plane to Raleigh, North Carolina, and taken to a research institute, where workers use an old cigarette machine to roll the harvest into thick, tightly wound government-issue joints.

The Oxford farm is well known around town. On summer nights, the smell of the marijuana harvest wafts temptingly over the security fence. Creative would-be thieves have cast fishing lines over the barrier, hoping to reel in a juicy leaf or bud. Some former workers have confessed to smuggling out some of the government's stash, while others say they simply ate some of the harvest while on duty. Workers at the farm have a sense of

Ole Miss Marijuana

Harvests are good.

ernment monopoly" is Randall's critique of the government's weed. "I'm used to it. I mean, it works. I'm not concerned if it's got that lovely Panama taste."

humor about it all. They've been known to send joyful Christmas greetings signed "The Ole Miss Marijuana Project."

Patients who receive the handiwork from the pot farm say that the government's pot is nothing special. Some say that because the joints are frozen before being shipped out, the pot is too dry and, therefore, hard to smoke. One user puts the government pot in a plastic bag with lettuce, so it absorbs moisture and makes it easier to smoke. "I'm not complaining," confesses stockbroker Irvin Rosenfield, "but it's not the best stuff." He has a rare disease that causes tumors on his bones, and uses marijuana to ease muscle and joint pain. "It's what you might expect from a gov-

Patients who receive the handiwork from the pot farm say that the government's pot is nothing special. Some say that because the joints are frozen before being shipped out, the pot is too dry and, therefore, hard to smoke.

A day in the life of the government's Oxford, Mississippi, pot farm.

> After evaluating volumes of testimony, the DEA's chief administrative law judge, Francis L. Young, ruled that marijuana should be reclassified to allow its medicinal use. "By any measure of rational analysis," Young concluded, "marijuana can be safely used within a supervised routine of medical care."

The Medical Question Debated

Several groups sued the government in 1972 to have marijuana reclassified to make it legal for medicinal use. This case lingered for years before the DEA finally held hearings in the late 1980s. After evaluating volumes of testimony, the DEA's chief administrative law judge, Francis L. Young, ruled that marijuana should be reclassified to allow its medicinal use. "By any measure of rational analysis," Young concluded, "marijuana can be safely used within a supervised routine of medical care." He also called marijuana "one of the safest therapeutically active substances known to man." To deny it to patients who needed it would be "unreasonable, arbitrary, and capricious," he added. But what about the arguments that legalizing marijuana as a medicine would confuse a public bombarded with messages that marijuana is an evil weed? That shouldn't prevent sick patients from getting the medicine they needed, Young declared, stating that "the fear of sending such a signal cannot be permitted to override the legitimate need."

These positive words about marijuana, emanating from the heart of an agency dedicated to eradicating it, sent a wave of panic through anti-drug forces. It wasn't long before a counterattack was launched. Despite Young's carefully studied opinion, the DEA overruled his decision and put a stop to plans for rescheduling marijuana and making it available as a medicine. The following year, the DEA's chief administrator Robert Bonner issued a 46-page ruling declaring that marijuana had no "currently accepted medical applications." Bonner ventured the novel idea that marijuana wasn't making people better—it was only a cruel illusion created by the effects of the drug: "Any mind-altering drug that produces euphoria can make a sick person think he feels better," Bonner proclaimed.

104

But this was a benefit "based on rationalizations caused by drug dependence, not on any medical benefits caused by the drug . . . Beyond doubt, the claims that marijuana is medicine are false, dangerous, and cruel. Sick men, women, and children can be fooled by these claims and experiment with the drug. Instead of being helped, they risk serious side effects." Needless to say, Bonner, not Judge Young, had the final word.

Prescription Refilled

The logistics of legalizing medicinal marijuana are still being worked out. Cultivating it for any form remains illegal, although some marijuana growers were eyeing medical marijuana as a way to make their operation more legitimate. They were placing a Geneva cross over their crops, hoping to convince police that they were growing a medicine, not an illegal weed. Medical marijuana was being sold at more than a half off normal street prices, causing officials to worry that crops allegedly bought for medicinal purposes would be diverted into the black market for a tidy profit.

Doctors were walking a fine line when it came to medical marijuana. A group of

Shawn Power (bottom row, third from left) is the world's longest living HIV positive hemophiliac who has medicated himself solely with marijuana.

Hot Box
To fill a room or car with marijuana smoke

Hempen Collar, Cravat, Necktie, Necklace, Garter or Halter

A hangman's noose, which was made with hemp rope

California physicians sued the government after they were threatened with losing their licenses for prescribing marijuana. A temporary settlement has created an uneasy truce between both sides, with doctors being allowed to prescribe it for a limited number of ailments, including cancer, AIDS, epilepsy, and multiple sclerosis. Meanwhile, the California Medical Association has issued guidelines to doctors to help them with this issue, suggesting that they tell patients of both the risks and the benefits of using it, and also reminding patients that marijuana remains an illegal substance under federal law.

The only legally available marijuana prescription is synthetic THC, pot's psychoactive component. It's called Marinol, and it's a Schedule II drug that was approved by the FDA for cancer treatment in 1985 and for AIDS in 1992. It's made by a small biotech company in suburban Chicago. Critics of this drug say that the medical benefits of marijuana are found in other compounds of the plant besides THC, and that these are not included in Marinol. Because many people seek marijuana to ease nausea, the prospect of swallowing a pill just doesn't work. It's easier for them to smoke real marijuana, which becomes active within minutes, as opposed to swallowing Marinol, which can take up to an hour to take effect.

Prince of Bel Air

One of the most unusual medical marijuana cases involves Todd McCormick, the so-called "Pot Prince of Bel Air." He was arrested at a mansion in this exclusive Los Angeles neighborhood and charged with growing more than four thousand marijuana plants. There is more than just a little irony to the fact that the house was located on Stone Canyon Road.

McCormick is a lifelong cancer sufferer who had taken marijuana to ease the painful effects of bone and spinal disease. He claims he was growing so many plants in order to test which ones were the most effective for different diseases. But a federal grand jury saw it another way. They charged McCormick and eight others with conspiracy and possession of marijuana for sale. Charged along with McCormick was publisher Peter McWilliams. His lawyer denied the charges and said that the indictments represent a government campaign to tarnish the medical marijuana movement. McWilliams, who has AIDS, says he is working with McCormick to publish a book on medical marijuana.

The Strongest Recommendation

Despite the many hurdles facing its implementation, the medical marijuana issue will not disappear for one vital reason: Patients believe it works. And they're not hesitant to tell others who may need it. Cancer patients speak of enduring wretched periods of nausea and then discovering a small stash of pot in their mailbox one day, courtesy of a concerned friend. As word spreads, the medicinal marijuana movement has gained momentum. The passage of state voter initiatives only brings into the open what had been an underground practice for years. This is a profound movement involving grandmothers and other mainstream citizens who just want to get well.

One campaign ad for California's medical marijuana initiative, Prop. 215, featured a nurse whose husband was fighting cancer but couldn't handle the intense nausea from his chemotherapy. "So I broke the law and got him marijuana. It worked. He could eat. He had an extra year of life," the long-time nurse told voters. "God forbid, someone you love may need it."

Similar heartbreaking stories appeared across the nation. In a *Good Housekeeping* magazine article in 1997, a mother confessed to breaking the law to save the life of her son. "We're the most normal family you could imagine. We mail in our taxes on time and always stop at red lights," the California mother began. Her 17-year-old son had Crohn's disease, and suffered from painful stomach inflammation. One day she noticed a marked improvement in his condition, and soon found out it was because he had been smoking marijuana. "I went ballistic," the mother recalls. But then she found out that marijuana was actually a perfect medicine for her son. He began using it with her blessing, and was able to resume a normal school life. "I'm just a mom who's doing

> In a *Good Housekeeping* magazine article in 1997, a mother confessed to breaking the law to save the life of her son. "We're the most normal family you could imagine. We mail in our taxes on time and always stop at red lights."

the best she can for her family. Because that's what moms do."

Marijuana laws put patients in a difficult position. They risk jail by taking medication they believe can make them better. A Los Angeles teacher, for example, says she turned to marijuana as a last resort to treat her eye problems. She was born with an underdeveloped optic nerve. Years of sophisticated medical treatment did little to improve her sight. Then some-one suggested she try marijuana. To her surprise, she found that it helped. Her vision improved so much that she began to see well enough to write a check for the first time in her life. Yet her joy is weighed down by the fact that she's breaking the law. "I'm in such a dilemma," she said with anguish, beginning to cry. Meanwhile, she's worried that she could lose her teaching job because of her marijuana use. She also has to deal with teaching her students about the dangers of marijuana, while not being able to tell them that this same drug is the very medicine making it possible for her to see. "What can I do?" she asks. "The choice is to see or not to see. Have you any other medicine?"

Viewing marijuana as a medicine casts it in a provocative new light. The medical marijuana campaign has been nothing less than a pounding headache for anti-drug forces. It's one thing to oppose marijuana for recreational use. In that battle, anti-drug forces take the moral high ground. But things get dicey when it comes to denying critically ill patients the medicine they need to get well. Elevating the marijuana weed to the status of medicine adds another level of controversy to the already contentious plant. It pits patients appreciative of marijuana's healing aspects against a government and anti-drug forces who prefer that the plant's benevolent side remain hidden.

Alice B. Toklas
Marijuana brownie

Bite One's Lips or Boot the Gong
To smoke marijuana

Lipton's
Weak marijuana that only gets you as buzzed as the tea would

Bomber, Fatty, Doobee, Zol, J, etc.
A marijuana cigarette

marijuana
lab report

stoned in the name of science

the U.S. military was eager to enlist hemp as an ally during World War II, but it had a serious problem. Federal drug officials had already outlawed the hemp plant in the form of marijuana. But hemp was badly needed to make rope and canvas for the war effort. So the government turned to Dr. H.E. Warmke.

In a Cold Springs Harbor, New York, science station in 1943, Dr. Warmke toiled at a vital but peculiar research project. The experiment was reported by *Popular Science* magazine under the dramatic headline "Plant Wizards Fight Wartime Drug Peril." Dr. Warmke's challenge was to breed a strain of hemp with wonderful

Warmke discovered...that when a minnow is placed in a beaker with strong marijuana, "it soon is most thoroughly dead, and such an observation cannot be disputed."

fiber but no intoxicant punch in its leaves. Or, as the magazine article asks in its subtitle, "Can We Grow Hemp Without Dope?" Not wishing to create a breed of plant that would produce, as the article warned, "a drug that makes depraved creatures of its addicts," Warmke enlisted the aid of the lowly Atlantic minnow.

To test the potency of the marijuana plants, Warmke simply dropped unfortunate minnows into beakers filled with water and marijuana extract. The faster the fish died, the stronger the pot, he concluded. He then set aside the weaker marijuana strains for future breeding, while discarding the stronger stuff. In effect, Warmke was doing the opposite of what marijuana connoisseurs would do years later when they experimented to breed the most potent strains of the plant.

While Warmke never did discover his dopeless hemp, he did achieve a rarity in marijuana science: He reached a conclusion no one refuted. Warmke discovered, the magazine reported, that when a minnow is placed in a beaker with strong marijuana, "it soon is most thoroughly dead, and such an observation cannot be disputed."

No Lab Consensus

Warmke is just one of dozens of scientists who have brought marijuana into a laboratory. Hundreds of studies have attempted to measure everything from the psychological effects of the pot high to the long-term health consequences of heavy use. Stoned subjects have had their memories tested, their motor skills evaluated, and their lungs probed. Others have merely been observed to see how much they eat while suffering attacks of the munchies. The net result of all this lab work is that most of the data on marijuana is inconclusive. A good part of it, in fact, is contradictory. Some researchers

conclude that marijuana use turns people violent, while others say it makes them passive. Some say marijuana is a stepping-stone to other drug use, while others denounce this as myth. One researcher got so caught up in the confusion that he seemed to offer contradictory statements about his own research in a 1981 article published by *Science News*. Sociologist Richard Clayton at the University of Kentucky was quoted as stating, "I'm not saying that marijuana use invariably leads to heroin use or to cocaine use." A paragraph later he added, "I think that there's absolutely clear evidence that marijuana use is a stepping stone to other illicit drug use."

In 1972, the National Institute of Mental Health concluded in its annual Marijuana and Health Report that the question of whether marijuana was dangerous was very much up in the air: "Despite the advances of the past year, any simple answer to this disarmingly simple question is not likely to be possible in the future."

Marijuana research is challenging, sometimes for obvious reasons: Stoned people don't always follow instructions well even in social situations, never mind a laboratory setting. A researcher in 1958

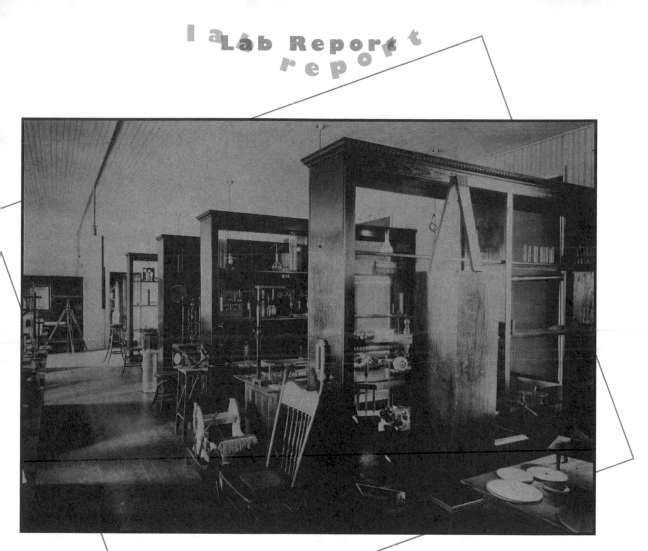

The laboratory where Dr. H.E. Warmke discovered the truth about minnows and marijuana.

observed high subjects and described them as having "an inability to recall what had just happened, so that the subject was often totally unable to sustain a conversation unless prompted about a recent remark by the observer . . . When the user wishes to explain what he had thought, there is only confusion."

A 1934 study told of one subject who "laughs uncontrollably and explosively for brief periods of time without the slightest provocation. If there is a reason it quickly fades, the point of the joke is lost immediately. Speech is rapid and flighty." It's no wonder that scientists have opted to use animal subjects instead of people. Creatures who have been stoned in the name of science include dogs, mice, rats, baboons, horses, bats, pigeons, and sea urchins.

A major challenge for early marijuana researchers was that its potency varied so greatly. That made it difficult to control doses to subjects, and to relate one

Creatures who have been stoned in the name of science include dogs, mice, rats, baboons, horses, bats, pigeons, and sea urchins.

experiment to another. Even if the marijuana was comparable, smoking it gave subjects different amounts, depending on how they inhaled. Much of the early research with marijuana is flawed because of these factors. Just as scientists were working on setting up more reliable research guidelines, the supply of marijuana dried up. A 1970 federal law severely restricted the flow of marijuana for research, creating an information void that could be exploited by political forces opposed to marijuana use.

One scientist who encountered difficulties with marijuana research was Andrew Weil, a doctor, writer, and educator with a sizable following as an icon of alternative healthcare. As a Harvard Medical School student in 1968, Weil designed one of the first controlled marijuana experiments. After haggling with the Federal Bureau of Narcotics, Weil and two associates began their study—not at Harvard, which didn't want to host the controversial project, but across the Charles River at Boston University. The study compared the effects of marijuana smoking on two groups—heavy users and those who had never gotten high. The research dispelled some early myths about marijuana smoking, including beliefs that it caused pupil dilation and low blood sugar. Regular users also scored higher on cognitive tests while stoned, not lower, as some would have predicted. The researchers made the interesting discovery that most first-time users didn't get high.

Weil concluded that marijuana didn't cause serious medical or psychological problems, although he declined to come out for legalizing it. Weil's conclusion that marijuana didn't lead to more serious drug use—the cornerstone of much anti-marijuana rhetoric at the time—caused a great stir. The marijuana study stigmatized Weil during his early professional career. He later expressed frustration with the lack of marijuana research by stating, "Administrators of scientific and government institutions feel marijuana is dangerous. Because it is dangerous, they are reluctant to allow work to be done on it. Because no work is done, people think it is dangerous."

Love Boat
Marijuana dipped in formaldehyde.

> **Andrew Weil's research dispelled some early myths about marijuana smoking, including beliefs that it caused pupil dilation and low blood sugar. Regular users also scored higher on cognitive tests while stoned, not lower, as some would have predicted.**

Stoned Measurements

For decades, scientists have been fascinated with what happens to people when they're high on marijuana. In 1913, three American doctors familiar with cannabis as a medicinal extract decided to sample their supply. They set out on a roller coaster journey, based on their report in the *Journal of the American Pharmaceutical Association*: "About one hour after taking the drug a pleasurable sensation was experienced which can be described only as one of well-being and complete satisfaction . . . About two hours after taking the drug, an uncomfortable feeling was experienced, followed shortly by nausea and vomiting." One doctor looks at another and observes him with a "slight twitching of the corners of the mouth . . . Presently he broke out into a restrained but hearty laugh."

Later, after a quiet card game, the three, "without any comment, assumed as comfortable a position as possible and fell into a doze." Their conclusion: "No two persons can be expected to exhibit the same symptoms as a result of ingesting equal quantities of the same drug, and no person can be depended upon to react in exactly the same manner from the same drug on different occasions."

A 1934 study, for example, observed subjects who experienced "anxiety within 10 to 30 minutes after smoking . . . often accompanied by panic states and even fear of death. Later, calmness euphoria . . . exhilaration." The high from marijuana smoking has been found to be so subjective, in fact, that researchers in 1970 discovered an interesting effect with a placebo. Told that they would be given two joints to smoke, some subjects were given a placebo instead. "They indicated that they were high and some actually became quite stimulated from the placebo ...When the same individuals received the test marijuana cigarette in the next testing session, they commented that this marijuana was much more 'potent' than that which they had received the first time."

Bogart
To hog the joint

Politics vs. Medicine

In the past century, there have been four comprehensive studies on the effects of marijuana. All have concluded that moderate marijuana use is not dangerous. Not surprisingly, political forces have protested these findings.

In 1893, the British government formed the Indian Hemp Drugs Commission to evaluate the problem of marijuana in India. It was an exhaustive study that involved interviews with more than 1,000 witnesses, including 335 doctors. The research team visited more than 30 cities to collect evidence. The commission concluded that hemp drug use did not lead to violent crime, and that moderate use did not pose serious health risks.

In 1925, the U.S. military convened a study of marijuana use by soldiers stationed at the Panama Canal Zone. The military wanted to know if it should ban its sale there. The study revealed that alcohol was more to blame for troop delinquency. Researchers concluded, "There is no evidence that marijuana as grown here is a 'habit-forming' drug...or that it has any appreciable deleterious influence on the individual using it." No marijuana prohibition was necessary, the study concluded. Military brass, unhappy with these results, simply commissioned another study. After further review, however, researchers made the same conclusion in 1933. Despite this, marijuana sales were banned in the Canal Zone.

In 1944, the "La Guardia Report" concluded that marijuana use was not addictive, nor did it cause mental instability, sexual deviance, or criminal misconduct.

The La Guardia Report

Probably one of the most interesting major marijuana studies was the New York Mayor's Committee on Marijuana, which became known as the "La Guardia Report" when it was published in 1944. The comprehensive study of marijuana use in New York City debunked many of the negative myths that had dogged pot users for years. The researchers concluded that marijuana use was not addictive, nor did it cause mental instability, sexual deviance, or criminal misconduct.

117

Harry Anslinger, head of the Federal Bureau of Narcotics at the time, attacked the committee's findings in an editorial published in the *Journal of the American Medical Association*: "Public officials will do well to disregard this unscientific, uncritical study and continue to regard marijuana as a menace wherever it is purveyed." He also called it a "government-printed invitation to youth and adults—above all teenagers—to go ahead and smoke all the reefers they feel like."

As part of its report, the committee noted the social climate of the time regarding marijuana use. Researchers pointed to pamphlets as well as high-strung newspaper accounts that depicted marijuana as a "killer drug" and "loco weed" that would produce a "delirious rage which sometimes leads to high crime, such as assault and murder." The report quotes from an article in the *New York Daily Worker* that depicted marijuana users as being on the road to "insanity, robberies, thrill murders, sex crimes and other offenses."

To see what was really happening where New Yorkers were lighting up, researchers headed into the field to find out. They sent six undercover police officers into the five

hundred known "tea pads" around town—apartments where pot parties were being held. This research provides an incredibly detailed look at how marijuana was used recreationally during this time.

Three grades of marijuana were available on the street in those days, starting with the low-grade, American-grown "sassfras," which cost 50 cents for 3 cigarettes. That was followed by the "panatela" cigarette from South America, and finally the supreme "Gungeon" variety, rumored to be from Africa, that sold for a buck a reefer.

Tea pads of the day were eerily similar to what two decades later would be the design of choice as hangouts for toking hippies: "The tea pad . . . has comfortable furniture, a radio . . . The lighting is more or less uniformly dim, with blue predominating. An incense burner is considered part of the furnishings. The walls are frequently decorated with pictures of nude subjects suggestive of perverted sexual practice."

The report goes on to describe a relaxed atmosphere with regulars engaging in conversations. Tea pad regulars talked of how marijuana made them feel adequate, and eased their "mental conflicts." Contrary to popular belief, tea pad

Music was a key component of the Tea Pad scene.

regulars weren't interested in any wild orgies. Even marijuana consumed in brothels, which were also studied by the La Guardia report, didn't appear to increase eroticism. In tea pads with sexually provocative pictures on the wall, it is the undercover cop who ends up staring at them, not the tea pad regulars.

As part of its clinical study, the New York research team observed 72 prison inmates from Riker's, Hart Island, and a women's penitentiary. These prisoners were given up to eight joints an hour. The marijuana gave them a "sense of well-being, contentment and cheerfulness." Not surprisingly, having smoked such a large amount of marijuana, the prisoners exhibited confusion during tests.

The researchers took the bold step of re-creating the party atmosphere of a tea pad on the final night of the experiment with prison smokers. Perhaps it was some

Spreading the Bad News

Anti-pot forces don't often mention these major studies when they lecture about the evils of marijuana. Fortunately for them, they don't have to. The federal government, with a vested interest in convincing the public that marijuana is dangerous, has funded hundreds of other studies in order to build its case against the plant. And the federal government makes sure to publicize and promote any study that infers the evils of marijuana use. For example, at the National Conference on Marijuana Use in 1995,

kind of reward for the subjects. They were consulted about how they wanted the room to look. Like home owners reviewing plans with a contractor, they hashed out the entire design, from lighting to music to what kinds of floor cushions. The subjects were allowed as many reefers as they wanted. Researchers reported that the subjects "crowded around with their hands outstretched like little children begging for candy." Some of them took a dozen. What happened? Basically, everyone partied quietly for a couple of hours, snacked on bread and jam, and ultimately went to bed. The study concluded: "The publicity concerning the catastrophic effects of marijuana smoking in New York City is unfounded."

> **The subjects were allowed as many reefers as they wanted. Researchers reported that the subjects "crowded around with their hands outstretched like little children begging for candy." Some of them took a dozen. What happened? Basically, everyone partied quietly for a couple of hours, snacked on bread and jam, and ultimately went to bed.**

Donna Shalala, secretary of Health and Human Services, trumpeted a new study that provided a hint that marijuana might be addictive. This point is highly controversial, but it's one that anti-marijuana forces desperately need in order to convince the public that marijuana is dangerous.

The National Institute on Drug Abuse trumpeted the news, which involved a study by scientists at the Scripps Research Institute. Researchers found that rats injected with doses of THC produced the chemical corticotropin, a signifier of addiction withdrawal. Still, researchers admitted there was no "direct evidence" to call pot a hard drug, while also stating that traces of corticotropin in the brains of the rats could have been caused by the stress of being immobilized for the study.

Major Findings

Early researchers had a simple question about marijuana: Could it kill? They decided that dogs would be sacrificed to determine the answer. Dog subjects were common in marijuana research in the late nineteenth and early twentieth centuries. These studies determined that when given regular doses, dogs showed an initial period of excitability, followed by some awkward moments of stumbling. Then they appeared drowsy, usually opting for a nap.

One study was designed to see if a massive amount of marijuana would kill a 25-pound dog. The scientists were in for a surprise. The stoned pooch, although unconscious for a day and a half, recovered completely. The researchers tripled the dose with another dog and observed the same result, with the canine going into a prolonged marijuana stupor and then emerging his old spunky self two days later. Had these researchers had the benefit of modern reports on marijuana overdoses, they probably could have saved these lab dogs a lot of trauma. There is probably no fatal dose of marijuana. To literally get a killer buzz, a marijuana smoker would have to inhale a hundred pounds of marijuana per minute for 15 minutes.

Studies have also shown that marijuana doesn't kill over the long run either. The results of a recent study by San Francisco researcher Stephen Sidney showed that long-time pot users did not have a higher rate of death than nonusers. Similar studies of long-term users in Greece, Costa Rica, and Jamaica have yielded the same conclusion.

But marijuana smoking takes its toll on health and mental function. There is evidence that marijuana use may depress the body's immune system, but no conclusive finding. Studies have also documented marijuana's negative effect on short-term memory, and there are indications that this impairment may last well after users stop toking. Researchers have also found that marijuana smoking damages the lungs in a similar way that tobacco smoking does, including promoting cell changes that may be precancerous, and leads to higher rates of lung infections and other respiratory problems.

One study was designed to see if a massive amount of marijuana would kill a 25-pound dog. The scientists were in for a surprise. The stoned pooch, although unconscious for a day and a half, recovered completely.

Social Studies

Hundreds of marijuana studies have been designed to illustrate the social consequences of marijuana use. Researchers have tried to prove that marijuana smokers are poor drivers, bad employees, forgetful, and otherwise antisocial. At best, though, study results have often been contradictory.

A 1994 study by the National Highway Traffic Safety Administration that examined almost two thousand accidents in seven states concluded that "there was no indication that cannabis by itself was a cause of fatal crashes." The report also noted that alcohol impairs driving to a far greater extent. But a recent report issued by NIDA claimed that marijuana definitely impairs driving skills. However, a closer look at this study reveals that stoned subjects were not given a driving exam but a field sobriety test. Marijuana subjects given two joints to inhale were twice as likely to goof up when attempting to touch their finger to their nose. They also had more difficulty balancing on one leg for 30 seconds.

NIDA pointed to a study involving 4,600 municipal workers in Texas that identified marijuana smokers as workers with worse

attitudes than their straight peers. The study concluded that marijuana smokers were less likely to be committed to the organization, experienced low job satisfaction, and had less faith in management.

Another study that questioned the work ethic of marijuana smokers involved rats. The 1972 study found that rats trained to fetch water reduced their work output almost to zero while under the influence of marijuana. Humans have also shown similarly dismal performances in lab tests, often growing bored with simple tasks assigned to them. In one study testing motor skills, one distracted subject was observed "drawing patterns on the

A sociological study in 1968 found that college-age pot smokers were more likely to oppose "the traditional, established order." The study also said marijuana tokers were more likely to instead live by a "hang-loose" creed.

123

oscilloscope screen with a dot of light he controlled." Another subject was so disinterested in the tedious tasks assigned to him while stoned, that he amused himself by blowing into a microphone and making feedback sounds.

In a study of motivation and marijuana smoking—another controversial area of study—a researcher at the University of Texas tested pot users to see how hard they'd work to earn an extra dime. After emerging stoned from a lab smoking booth, subjects were told they could "work" by pushing a button that would produce successive payouts of 10 cents. While some might say wisdom might stop subjects from working for such low wages, the researcher concluded that "marijuana produced a decline in the amount of time spent in the working component...and caused subjects

to exit the work component earlier." The study concluded that the effects of marijuana on motivation were not predictable.

A sociological study in 1968 found that college-age pot smokers were more likely to oppose "the traditional, established order." The study also said marijuana tokers were more likely to instead live by a "hang-loose" creed.

Pot, the Social Drug

While the conventional wisdom is that pot smokers drift off into their own inner thoughts, studies have shown that the opposite is true—in lab animals as well as people. A 1969 study involved albino rats kept inside a three-foot square box. Their only source of amusement was a tiny opening through which they could observe another rat or a hamster. The researchers noted that the drugged rats showed more

Another study that questioned the work ethic of marijuana smokers involved rats in 1972. The study found that worker rats trained to fetch water reduced their work output almost to zero while under the influence of marijuana.

curiosity and spent more time looking in at their neighbor. They also visited the other animals when it was allowed.

A 1987 study at Johns Hopkins University in Baltimore put pot users into a residential lab for almost three weeks. They smoked up to four joints a day, including three during a crucial afternoon period when they had the option of visiting with neighbors. Pot users, it turns out, were social butterflies compared to their straight counterparts. Rather than lay around in a drug stupor, they preferred the company of others while stoned.

The image of pot users as social animals was also reinforced by a 1993 study of college students cavorting on Halloween. That study found a connection between marijuana use and the tendency of students to "masquerade with a group."

Mezz Roll
Well packed joint with
a large diameter

The Chocolate Buzz

While scientists have been unable to account for how marijuana triggers intense food cravings, otherwise known as the munchies, one clue comes from a 1996 study on the effects of chocolate on the brain. Turns out that chocoholics and pot heads have something in common.

Eating a chocolate delight and getting high affect the same part of the human brain, according to research from San Diego's Neuroscience Institute. Chemicals in chocolate, in fact, stimulate the brain in much the same way that the THC of pot does, only in a greatly reduced effect. Because THC has a much more profound effect, the buzz from one candy bar is not as easily felt. A 130-pound person would have to eat 25 pounds of chocolate to get a similar pot high. Still, the research explains why chocoholics and pot users seek solace in their respective vices—both items elevate mood.

Lung Explorer

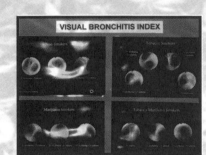

VISUAL BRONCHITIS INDEX

The smell of marijuana smoke wafting from the UCLA Medical Center office of Donald Tashkin might give colleagues the wrong idea. It's not that he's throwing pot parties. In fact, some of the research he's done through the years may dampen the spirits of pot smokers because of what it reveals about potential lung damage.

Tashkin has been studying the effects of marijuana smoke on the lungs for almost two decades, certainly one of the nation's longest studies of its kind. It was a topic that at first didn't hold much interest for him. He was called in to investigate the effects of marijuana smoking in the late 1970s as part of a much larger federally funded study of marijuana's psychological

Donald Tashkin, head of UCLA's pulmonary lab, has studied the effects of marijuana smoke on the lungs for almost two decades.

effects. Tashkin, head of UCLA's pulmonary lab, thought the study was a no-brainer. "My expectation was that marijuana smoking would cause some abnormality in lung function," Tashkin recalls during an interview at his UCLA office. "I was very surprised to find that marijuana did the opposite—it actually opened up the airways in the lungs rather than constricting them. That piqued my interest and has sustained it ever since."

Tashkin first set out to develop an asthma medicine containing THC. He had some success, but ultimately concluded that other medicines were better. In 1982, he began a federally funded study on the long-term effects of marijuana smoking on the lungs, a project that continues to this day. He had no trouble recruiting volunteers, easily finding about 135 regular pot smokers who inhale between three to four joints per day. His study compares these Herculean tokers with heavy ciga rette smokers, smokers of both pot and tobacco, and nonsmokers. He's probed their lungs with tubes and assorted measuring devices, and also monitored symptoms ranging from coughs to wheezing to bronchitis. He's concluded that marijuana smokers face many of the same lung impairments that cigarette smokers endure, including persistent cough, phlegm, increased frequency of bronchitis, and other lung ailments. He's also detected precancerous changes in the lungs of marijuana smokers similar to those of cigarette smokers.

Tashkin says that because he's studying the potential health consequences of marijuana, he's had an easier time in getting federal support than researchers looking into possible medicinal uses for pot. Still, it was not easy getting his grant. "It does require going through some regulatory hoops," he observes. He needed approval from the Drug Enforcement Agency, the Food and Drug Administration, UCLA, and California officials before he could even approach the National Institute on Drug Abuse for a grant. The process took two years. "You're bucking tradition to try and obtain that permission for therapeutic studies. But if you're using it to investigate health effects . . . you can see that it would be easier," he admits. Tashkin, however, believes that the federal government should allow easier access to research on the use of marijuana as a medicine. "Yes, it should, because it's being used that way, whether the government likes it or not," he states.

Tashkin thinks that marijuana shows great promise in the area of pain relief and reducing inflammation. He has great reservations, however, in smoked marijuana being used in the two most common ways it is being administered as a medicine—to treat AIDS and cancer patients. Tashkin says that studies have shown that marijuana inhibits the lung's immune cells, putting patients with an already suppressed immune function at even greater risk. And in mice studies, he's observed that THC causes cancerous tumors to grow at a faster rate. "If you give someone marijuana to combat the nausea and vomiting of chemotherapy, you might enhance the tumor. That defeats the purpose of the chemotherapy," he states.

Far Out Research

While a majority of marijuana research is deadly serious, a segment of it stands out because of its startling irrelevance or painfully obvious conclusions. For example, one study determined that marijuana-smoking employees were less likely to support company drug testing or drug-free workplace programs. Another study reported that those fun-loving swingers from the 1970s were more liberal about their sexuality and more likely to favor marijuana legalization.

For some reason, researchers at the Buffalo School of Medicine released their finding that sea urchins do indeed have receptors for the THC component of marijuana. They have them, all right—in their sperm. Meanwhile, the issue of whether marijuana is an aphrodisiac is still being debated.

In 1976, three researchers got two baboons high—first at ground level and then at higher elevations. Their conclusion? At higher altitudes, stoned baboons did less work. The moral of the story: Don't expect much of an effort from an elevated stoned baboon.

Several studies examining the munchies have yielded results that even a casual toker could have predicted. In 1989, a behavioral scientist at Johns Hopkins School of Medicine put six stoned adult men in the same room as a bounty of candy bars, potato chips, cookies, pudding, and sodas. Then they sat back and watched the calories fly. What would probably make for a funny comedy skit was instead a research project at a respected medical school. The subjects were given four joints a day, and, well, there was that junk-food stash nearby with little else to do. On

> **In 1976, three researchers got two baboons high first at ground level and then at higher elevations. Their conclusion? At higher altitudes, stoned baboons did less work. The moral of the story: Don't expect much of an effort from an elevated stoned baboon.**

average, they gained six pounds over a 13-day period. Researchers, of course, gained the fact that marijuana smokers will probably eat junk food if it's handy.

As part of the "La Guardia Report," researchers tried to test whether pot users laughed more than sober people. To do this, a monitor had subjects listen to a Jack Benny radio program on two Sunday evenings—once while they were straight and once when they were stoned. The amount of laughter on these days was then compared to the length and frequency of the laughter of the actual studio audience. Still with us? The researchers concluded that, "without the drug, the subjects laughed, roughly speaking, only half as often and as long as the audience, while under the drug they laughed almost as often and the laugh time was about 75 percent that of the audience." The conclusion after this study, a result no doubt experienced countless times outside the lab, was that high people "laugh more readily and for longer time intervals."

It's hard to imagine there was much laughter when subjects of a bizarre 1978 marijuana study found out what they had been smoking in the lab. Wishing to test the smelling ability of marijuana users, researchers had subjects smoke placebos

rolled with human hair. Smelling seemed to be impaired. One of the more unusual findings from this study was that subjects appeared to get more high from smoking the hair-filled placebos than real marijuana joints.

While no one has directly tied marijuana use to watching TV's *The X-Files*, a 1993 study indicates that pot smoking may be an indication of a belief in psychic phenomenon. Sixty-nine percent of what the study identified as 150 "experienced" marijuana smokers had telepathic moments while stoned. Meanwhile, half of them reported seeing auras and taking journeys via out-of-body experiences. Three-quarters of them believed in ESP, and many thought they were psychic.

Yes, the truth is out there. But will it ever be known? Scientists are probably more sure of what marijuana does to animals than how it affects people. The marijuana research that has been done on human subjects, rather than producing accepted truths based on hard science, only generates more debate about the always controversial plant.

Lab Excesses

There aren't official records kept for it, but the most marijuana ever smoked was probably done under laboratory settings. Several marijuana studies are notable for the quantity of pot consumed by the subjects. In 1975, a group of macaque monkeys were fed the equivalent of 20 joints a day for 2 years, presented to them in spiked raisin cookies and prunes. With such a buzz, the monkeys cut back on social interaction, and some females became more aggressive. The heavy buzz did little to diminish the sex drive of the monkeys.

A U.S. Public Health study in 1946 at a Lexington, Kentucky, hospital allowed 6 marijuana "addicts" to smoke 17 joints a day for more than a month. "At first, the marijuana smokers showed extreme exhilaration," *Newsweek* magazine reported. "They talked, laughed and pranced about the room . . . After a few days, they grew lethargic and careless about personal hygiene." The article pointed out that the heavy tokers "sulked when subjected to exhaustive mental and physical tests."

In another mammoth smoke-out, male subjects being observed for changes in their sex organs due to marijuana use began slowly with one joint. They increased that consumption by 1 a day until they were up to 10. Then they just went for it. "Four of the five smokers," researchers observed, "had no difficulty smoking at least 10 cigarettes, and most smoked far more than this daily with a maximum of 31 in one day . . . One smoker had difficulty in maintaining this level."

hemp

the soybean of the 21st century

at an indoor mall in Santa Monica, California, the food court is an expected sight, as are the many shoe, clothing, gift, and gadget stores. The huge marijuana leaf painted on a store window, however, is a surprise. It's part of a promotional display for one of the mall's showcase stores, located right off the central escalator.

If this were winter, in fact, the storefront's robust leaf would face out on Santa's village, flashing thousands of wide-eyed kids. But this is summer. The popular shopping center is filled with tourists straight from the beach on the requisite gift hunt, as well as locals rummaging for bargains or munching assorted mall cuisine. What these mall wanderers will discover, if they venture past the leaf and into the store, is that they've come face-to-face with one of the retail world's hottest buying trends.

This amazing market star is none other than marijuana's botanical cousin, the sober-minded hemp.

The promotional leaf is courtesy of the Body Shop, the retail chain selling a hip line of lotions, oils, and soaps. Known for introducing unconventional fruity fragrances to the world of skin care, the Body Shop was launching what some would say was its fruitiest line yet —moisturizers made from hemp. There was hemp soap, hand lotion, and even hemp lip conditioner.

Market watchers put hemp retail sales in the United States in the $50 million range in 1997, up from only a few million in 1993.

Knowing full well that its customers would have a few questions, the store was distributing a handy brochure that spelled out the basics. "It's a Plant, not a Weed," the booklet declares. And a very special weed at that. "The most useful plant known to humankind," the brochure gushes—the one with 25,000 uses. It also contains an ingredient of interest to those with dry skin: moisturizing fatty acids. Company founder Anita Roddick, who's seen a lot of moisturizers in her day, tried out hemp and moved it right to the head of the class: "The best oil for dry skin that I've ever seen," she concluded. The new lotions are now being spread on hands across America, jumping to almost 10% of the Body Shop's U.S. sales.

These lotions make up only a small part of the hemp revolution. Hemp is everywhere. Hemp shirts are making bold fashion statements, letters are being penned on hemp stationary, and health-minded snackers are crunching away on honey-coated hemp seed treats. Creators of hemp seat covers rave about hemp's uncanny knack for holding its shape: "It doesn't wear out, it wears in!" Hemp seeds give ale a

A variety of soaps, lotions, and oils.

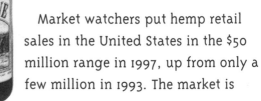

"The Kind Wine."

nice head, according to a microbrewer of a hemp ale. Meanwhile, vintners combined an unlikely pair—New York grapes and Amsterdam hemp—to produce Nirvana Homebrews, a hemp white wine. The makers encourage drinkers to "taste the essence."

Hemp is truly a miracle plant, according to its enthusiastic backers. The fiber is tough as nails, soft as cotton. Clothes made from hemp linen hang well. Hemp seeds make a nice pie crust. The seeds, and a cooking oil made from them, are healthy and nutritious, and have an exciting nutty flavor, reminiscent of hazelnut. Hemp seeds may boost your immune system. Chefs sprinkle hemp on salads, add it to cheeses or encrust it on fire-broiled fish. It is a new taste, and just a bit daring.

Market watchers put hemp retail sales in the United States in the $50 million range in 1997, up from only a few million in 1993. The market is

HEMPY'S
Sport & Travel Gear

Hemp travels well.

bags and jeans. His business has grown at a 15% rate for its first 5 years, a trend he expects to continue for the next decade or more. He's watched as the fledgling hemp industry stumbled along at the beginning, churning out inferior products, and sometimes failing to deliver at all. Now, he says, the industry has its act together, and it shows. Hemp is being hawked on Fifth Avenue in New York City and other fashionable shopping zones around the world. There are hundreds of manufacturers, and industry standards are improving. Big names have entered the game: Calvin Klein, Patagonia, Adidas, and Giorgio Armani are just a few of the brand names now offering hemp products. Walker proudly fingers a stylish button-down Patagonia shirt hanging smartly on a store rack. "It's a nice shirt, and it's environmental," he observes.

exploding, and the forecast is bright. Visionaries predict that it could reach as high as $10 billion by 2010.

A couple of blocks from the Body Shop in Santa Monica, along the city's trendy outdoor mall, Dean Walker has seen the maturation of the hemp industry during the 1990s. He's the owner of the Organic Cotton and Hemp Clothing store on the Third Street Promenade. The store offers everything from hemp soap to hemp travel

The future certainly looks bright for hemp,

and it couldn't have happened at a more provocative time. The public outcry to legalize marijuana for medicinal use is building to a crescendo. As anti-drug forces lament a rise in pot smoking by young Americans, along comes a marijuana relative with a cool sense of youth appeal.

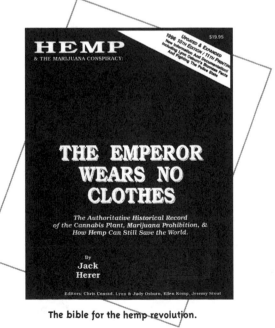

Herer suggests that a government-backed conspiracy in the 1930s led to the federal marijuana ban.

to the pro-marijuana movement. Hemp's long forgotten but significant history was revived by marijuana advocate Jack Herer, an outspoken campaigner for broader marijuana freedoms. A burly man who has been known to take mighty tokes off a pocket pipe during media interviews, Herer assembled a most compelling essay for legalizing marijuana in 1985, which he published as *The Emperor Wears No Clothes*. Despite its tabloid newspaper tone

Saving the Planet

To set the record straight, hemp is not exactly marijuana. They're the same plant, but because of genetics and cultivation techniques, they've developed different characteristics and are used very differently. Hemp has been grown for its fibrous stalk and nutritious seeds, while marijuana has been cultivated for the intoxicating quality of its leaves. Hemp is more lanky than marijuana, while marijuana has a fuller, bushy look. Industrial hemp, grown for centuries and used worldwide, has less than 1% THC, the psychoactive component of marijuana.

As a natural fiber and trendy consumer item, hemp has lent an added dimension

HEMP
& THE MARIJUANA CONSPIRACY:

1996 UPDATED & EXPANDED
New Information And Documentation!
Including Kyoto Treaty's Ramifications
And Fighting The Police State

$19.95

THE EMPEROR WEARS NO CLOTHES

The Authoritative Historical Record of the Cannabis Plant, Marijuana Prohibition, & How Hemp Can Still Save the World.

By
Jack
Herer

Editors: Chris Conrad, Lynn & Judy Osburn, Ellen Komp, Jeremy Stout

The bible for the hemp revolution.

Hemp hemp

Thomas Jefferson went out of his way to smuggle prized hemp seeds from China to plant back at Monticello; former president George Bush's life was saved by a hemp parachute when he jumped to safety in World War II; early drafts of the Declaration of Independence were written on hemp paper.

and crude cut-and-paste design, this book has become the bible for the modern hemp movement. It's Herer's loving tribute to the plant he believes will save the world. It provides a much more compelling argument for the legalization of marijuana than just having it around to smoke.

Herer suggests that a government-backed conspiracy in the 1930s led to the federal marijuana ban. He points to William Randolph Hearst and the DuPont chemical company as primary forces driving the anti-marijuana campaign, all to protect their own wood and chemical products from having to compete with hemp. The book delves into hemp's colorful history, and offers up some gems:

Mighty Mezz
An extremely potent marijuana cigarette

Jack Herer signing his tome.

135

Protesters rally around hemp.

lighting up, they would marvel at how hemp was going to save the planet. The hemp angle added much needed depth to the pro-marijuana movement.

The Next Level

From these crude beginnings, hemp has become a multimillion-dollar industry. Propelling the hemp movement today and taking it to the next level are people like the Organic Cotton and Hemp Store's Dean Walker. A former Green Peace worker, Walker has combined his passion for political activism with an entrepreneurial vision. His primary market is older and educated—consumers motivated to spend money on organic products and environmentally friendly goods. "We're a green retail business," Walker states. "We are not in the business of selling bongs and paraphernalia and rolling papers. We're selling this as an environmental product, as it really should be."

Thomas Jefferson went out of his way to smuggle prized hemp seeds from China to plant back at Monticello; former president George Bush's life was saved by a hemp parachute when he jumped to safety in World War II; early drafts of the Declaration of Independence were written on hemp paper.

Herer's book made for eye-opening reading among young marijuana advocates. Crude hemp items and literature promoting the plant began showing up at pro-pot rallies, music festivals, and other marijuana-friendly venues. Tie-dyed outfitted retro hippies began selling hemp clothes and jewelry to a sympathetic marijuana crowd, wowing them with stories from Herer's book. While

But others are boldly drawing the connection between marijuana and hemp. One company calls its soap product "Body Dope" and markets it under the slogan "Your daily dose." Manufacturers stitch

Alterna Hemp Shampoo ads were pulled from 106 Southern California bus benches because of their use of a cannabis leaf to promote their product.

marijuana leaves on their hemp clothing, or inscribe hemp hats with the playful message "Do Hemp." Law officials were making the connection, too. In August 1998, French police raided a Aix-en-Provence Body Shop store, whisking away hemp skin cremes and lotions. The *gendarmes* also confiscated the store's hemp literature.

Then, in November 1998, bowing to pressure from the anti-drug group DARE, Coast United Advertising pulled ads for Alterna Hemp Shampoo from 106 southern California bus benches because Alterna, Inc., used the image of a cannabis leaf to promote their hemp-based shampoo. The benches were pulled despite the fact that the ads clearly state that Alterna products are "THC (drug) free."

The U.S. Drug Enforcement Agency has taken a stern view of the burgeoning hemp industry, stating in a press release that "the cultivation of the marijuana plant exclusively for commercial and industrial purposes has many associated risks relating to diversion into the illicit drug traffic." Drug Czar Barry McCaffrey looks at hemp foods and clothing and sees more of the marijuana menace: "Legalizing hemp production," McCaffrey claims, "would be de facto legalization of marijuana cultivation." It's no coincidence that a resurgent anti-marijuana publicity campaign was launched just as the hemp movement was beginning to heat up. The United States remains the only industrialized nation not allowing hemp cultivation.

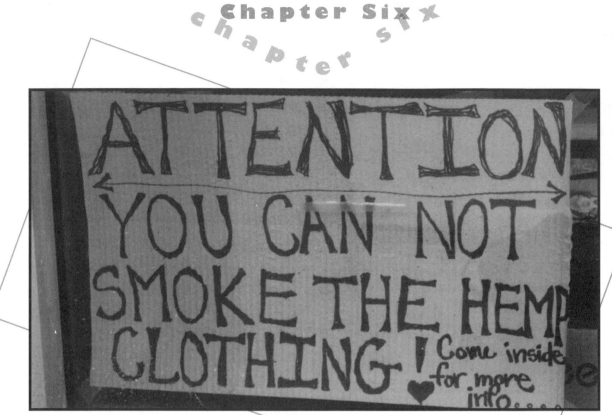

Sign in the window of the Organic Cotton Company.

Any association between hemp and marijuana irks Walker. "Some people will always say that this is a head shop," he notes sadly. And he's getting tired of the jokes, too: "We still get a lot of people in here who ask, 'Can we smoke your shirts?'" The owner of the Austin Hemp Company, Kelly Wilhite, has heard worse. Some customers are convinced that his hemp store is a front for drug dealers.

Many hemp entrepreneurs go out of their way to dissociate themselves from marijuana. But others, such as Craig Rubin, who owns a head shop offering hemp products and food in Los Angeles, is a proponent of both hemp and marijuana. In fact, he'd love to sell marijuana at his store—if the government would let him.

A study published in a marketing trade journal said consumers had a negative response to hemp's association with marijuana. Most said the association wouldn't make a hemp product more appealing, while a quarter of them said it might make them not want to buy the hemp item at all. They did, however, enjoy hearing about hemp's environmental plusses and its organic quality.

138

Researchers concluded: "Companies would be better off taking the high road to marketing—no pun intended."

Hemp may be difficult to hold back, no matter how it's promoted. It's the economy, stupid. Hemp meshes nicely with the emerging green consumer market. The hemp industry is expanding, Walker points out, right along with the organic foods industry. Consumers are willing to spend money on products that promote a healthier environment and a more organic lifestyle. This is the market where hemp's appeal really resonates. Unlike cotton, hemp can be successfully grown without pesticides. Cotton, in fact, is a notorious pesticide hog, making hemp an attractive alternative to consumers looking to make more organic selections at the market. Over time, hemp proponents predict that hemp will produce greater yields than cotton crops. Using hemp to make paper—as it was once uti-

lized—can save precious forests. Hemp supporters, including an official with the U.S. Department of Agriculture's alternative crop division, are hailing hemp as the "soybean of the new millennium."

Recreational hemp chair.

The United States remains the only industrialized nation not allowing hemp cultivation.

Chapter Six

A Plea from the Heartland

Unlike marijuana, which is usually promoted by the fringes of society, hemp is being touted from within the heartland of American society: its agrarian base. Kentucky farmers in 1998 sued the government for the right to grow hemp, arguing that it had no right to ban it because hemp is a different plant than marijuana. They are struggling to find an alternative to tobacco, their greatest cash crop. Research indicates that hemp could yield Kentucky farmers a profitable $1,200 an acre—not nearly as much as tobacco, but more than food crops such as corn, soybeans, and wheat. In Vermont, struggling dairy farmers were wondering, too, if hemp was the answer. They lobbied the state legislature to make hemp farming legal. There was opposition, of course, and the issue is fueling a hot political debate in Vermont. A congressional candidate spoke against the hemp movement there, saying it "sends the wrong message to our children." Elsewhere, however, several states ordered studies to evaluate the possibility of reviving their hemp crops. Republican Davis Monson successfully argued for a hemp study in North Dakota by declaring, "Hemp is as American as baseball and apple pie."

Hemp already has the mandatory celebratory spokespeople talking it up. Willie Nelson began preaching about the virtues of industrial hemp during the 1990s at Farm Aid concerts. He also launched his own line of hemp clothing. Meanwhile, actor Woody Harrelson was arrested planting hemp seeds in Kentucky. He's made a hemp fashion statement by taking a red-carpet stroll at the Academy Awards wearing a Giorgio Armani hemp tuxedo, accessorized with hemp shoes.

Republican Davis Monson successfully argued for a hemp study in North Dakota by declaring, "Hemp is as American as baseball and apple pie."

Ditch Weed
Inferior quality marijuana

One of many emerging catalog
companies where you can purchase
hip hemp products.

support your local
tobacco farmer
LEGALIZE HEMP

Hemp History

The history of hemp is long and colorful.
Hemp cultivation dates back five thousand
years. The Chinese used it to make fishing
nets and bow strings for their warrior
archers. It was also used as a lightweight
and inexpensive source for paper.
Egyptians employed hemp in construction
of the Pyramids, stuffing wet pieces of it
into huge rocks, which were broken open
as the fiber dried and swelled. Italians
called hemp the "substance of a hundred
operations," referring to its complicated
processing. It's a technique Venetians
mastered, creating a dominant hemp
industry during the sixteenth and seventeenth centuries.

During the fifteenth century, when
nations battled for control of major ocean
shipping routes, hemp played a vital
role in determining who would be the
dominating power. Spain, Holland,
England, and France all depended on a
quality hemp harvest to supply their naval
fleets with sails and rope. Hempen sails
carried Columbus and his crew to America.
The need for a dependable supply of hemp
was no idle concern. In 1533, King Henry
VIII ordered farmers to grow a specific
amount of hemp, an edict resurrected by

Very Superstitious

With so much riding on a successful hemp harvest, it's no wonder that some farmers resorted to unusual customs and superstitions to ensure a healthy crop. In France, it was considered a good omen for the hemp harvest if women were intoxicated on the first night of Lent. Not to miss out on the fun, French men yanked up the waistlines of their pants as high as they could while sowing hemp seeds, believing that their crop would one day grow as tall.

In some parts of France, it was believed that the relative height of the king and queen translated into the difference in the height of their male and female hemp plants. It was thus better if her royal highness was the taller of the two. In Germany, farmers leaped over bonfires after planting their hemp seeds, believing that the farmers jumping the highest would have the tallest hemp plants. Seeking divine assistance, some farmers only planted their hemp on holidays for long-legged saints, hoping that their plants would grow to be similarly tall.

Queen Elizabeth 30 years later. Meanwhile, Napoleon was so incensed that Russia was supplying hemp to England that he invaded Russia, hoping that by cutting off the hemp supply he would cripple the British fleet.

Early flags were made of hemp.

Golden Leaf
High quality marijuana

Hemp
hemp

Patriotic Potheads

George Washington and Thomas Jefferson were early American hempsters, but both lost money on the crop. Washington planted it at Mount Vernon in 1765, and mentioned it in a journal entry a year later, noting, "Began to separate the male from the Female Hemp...rather too late." Much hay has been made of this citation by pro-marijuana activists.

Washington's dismay at being tardy with the separation of the plant sexes is a lament often uttered by marijuana growers. This is because unfertilized

Washington was basically telling colonial farmers to forget about the lackluster European hemp and to go for the more intoxicating, resinous Indian variety.

female plants produce higher-potency marijuana. The implication of Washington's agricultural notation is that he's aiming to produce one heck of a marijuana crop. Before you can say, "But Washington didn't inhale," consider the further evidence that he implored other farmers in 1794 to "make the most you can of the Indian Hemp seed and sow it everywhere." Whether this was said in a gleeful marijuana haze is not certain, but it is known that Indian hemp was known for its intoxicant powers. Washington was basically telling colonial farmers to forget about the lackluster European hemp and to go for the more intoxicating, resinous Indian variety.

Jefferson was also a strong hemp advocate, prodding farmers to grow it as an alternative to tobacco. Jefferson didn't care much for tobacco, often calling it a "pernicious" drug, the very word that would later be used to condemn his beloved hemp. Jefferson saw hemp as an important crop for an independent nation because it provided a variety of products and could help employ many Americans.

Did he or didn't he?

143

He was so driven to increase the quality of American hemp that he even broke the law, smuggling prized hemp seeds from China into America. Jefferson also invented a special threshing machine for hemp processing.

Jefferson didn't care much for tobacco, often calling it a "pernicious" drug.

Revolutionary Fabric

While early drafts of the Declaration of Independence were written on hemp paper, it was the fiber itself that helped back up this bold statement. One way early colonialists shed their dependence from England was by refusing to send raw hemp fiber back to England. Americans instead began to process it themselves into valuable household products, including clothes and linen. Against the wishes of the British Crown, which forbid it, American women organized spinning bees and began working long into the night, turning raw fiber into usable thread and fabric, and weaving the clothes that would one day outfit the Revolutionary Army.

Early Pennsylvanians opened the first hemp paper factory in the seventeenth century. Hemp paper was made at a mill owned by Benjamin Franklin. Hemp was so vital that South Carolina voted to fund a hemp lobbyist to travel and promote hemp to its citizens, even sending him to Holland to bring back quality seeds for planting. One of America's earliest fighting ships, *Old Ironsides*, went to battle with hempen sails, rope, and rigging. There was enough of a market to foster hemp growing regions through the country. By 1810, hemp was a staple crop in Kentucky. Before the Civil War, there would be more than eight thousand hemp plantations there. Hemp growing spread to Tennessee, Wisconsin, and even California.

The sails, rope, and rigging for *Old Ironsides* were made of hemp. Anchors aweigh!

Hemp hemp

Hell of a Harvest

Hemp paper was made at a mill owned by Benjamin Franklin.

While hemp was a crucial crop, it was not a favorite with British and American colonial farmers ordered to grow it. For starters, hemp harvesting is back-breaking work. Farmers need to carefully prepare the soil, raking it several times. Seeds must be fresh and carefully selected. Colonial farmers who got their seeds shipped overseas by way of a long ocean journey sometimes received stale seeds that wouldn't produce the desired quality of fiber.

After planting a successful crop, farmers had to contend with the arduous tasks of the hemp harvest. And then there was the difficult job of processing the raw product into usable fiber. Early hemp farmers sometimes cut stands down by hand. Then they tied them into sheaths to prepare them for processing. Hemp needs to be "retted," a term which, as it sounds, is just another way of saying "rotted." This process removes the gummy coating that binds the usable fiber to the stalk. American farmers favored a retting method that often made their hemp less sturdy than European varieties. American

A hemp harvest in action.

145

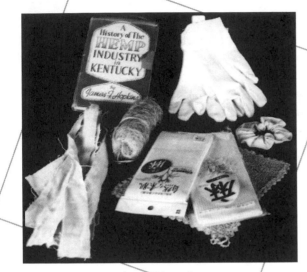
Historical hemp items.

Hemp Decline

The development of the cotton gin in 1893 made cotton America's dominant fiber, even though it was weaker, shorter, and rotted more easily than hemp. After the Civil War, U.S. hemp production fell off, and the industry never recovered. When tariffs for imported fibers were lifted in 1872, making other fibers a better buy, the domestic hemp crop began to falter. The most crucial reason hemp declined was that it couldn't compete with fibers from abroad, either at the high or low end. Even the American military preferred to spend higher prices for superior imported hemp. Beaten at the top by Russian and European hemp, American hemp was squeezed on the low side by inexpensive jute and other fibers used to make bagging and burlap. The rise of steam power in place of sails added another blow to hemp's demand.

farmers let their hemp harvest sit in the fields. Dew and winter moisture then loosened up the outer binding. Dew retting was inferior to the European method of water retting, which included immersing the crops in a stream for several days. Americans didn't like the stench of this process, and also feared that it might contaminate drinking supplies.

Once retted, hemp still poses challenges. Breaking the fiber from the stalk was once one of the hardest jobs a farmer or slave laborer would be asked to do. Tools and machinery were later invented to ease this burden.

Hemp seeds and oil.

146

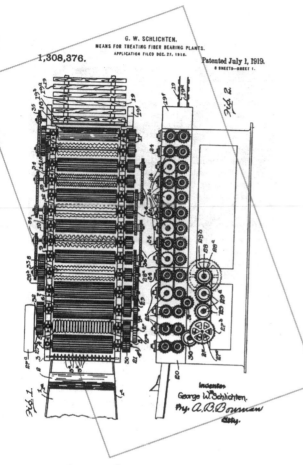

1,308,376.

G. W. SCHLICHTEN.
MEANS FOR TREATING FIBER BEARING PLANTS.
APPLICATION FILED DEC. 27, 1918.

Patented July 1, 1919.
8 SHEETS—SHEET 1.

The patent drawing for the Schlichten
Decorticator—hemp's cotton gin.

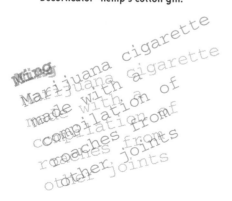

Billion-Dollar Crop

Hemp's demise was probably welcomed by farmers unhappy with all the hard work it took to harvest and process it. Dozens of innovators had come up with tools and machinery to make the job easier, but these only went so far. The machines were often expensive, removed too much of the valuable fiber, and yielded an inferior quality of hemp. But in the early 1900s, a new machine called a "decorticator" was hailed as the device that would revolutionize the hemp industry. Some predicted that the decorticator would do for hemp what the cotton gin did for cotton.

These pie-in-the-sky visions were set down on paper in a 1938 article in *Popular Mechanics* published under the provocative headline "New Billion-Dollar Crop." It was illustrated with pictures of a smiling woman outfitted in a hemp linen dress and swarthy sailors adjusting hemp rigging and sails. The article wasted no time in getting to the point: "American farmers are promised a new cash crop with an annual value of several hundred million dollars, all because a machine has been invented which solves a problem more than 6,000 years old."

The crop, of course, is hemp, a resurgent miracle crop that would lead Americans out of its depressed economy, providing thousands of jobs and saving Americans money on costly fabric imports that would now be made at home. The rest of the essay is a glowing tribute to hemp as the wonder crop that could be used to produce more than twenty-five thousand products, from towels to TNT. Yes, TNT. Resourceful manufacturers were using hemp hurds to make dynamite. It was also used for staples such as paper, overalls, and bed linen.

A 1954 marijuana tax stamp.

The article offered one cautionary note about the potential hemp boom, noting that the hemp plant also contains the marijuana blossom recently banned by federal law. But the magazine didn't foresee this as a stumbling block: "The connection of hemp as a crop and marijuana seems to be exaggerated. The drug is usually produced from wild hemp or loco-weed, which can be found on vacant lots and along railroad tracks in every state. If federal regulations can be drawn to protect the public without preventing the legitimate culture of hemp, this new crop can add immeasurably to American agriculture and industry."

As it turns out, this is one mighty "if." The 1937 Marijuana Tax Act did in fact spill over to the industrial hemp industry, driving farmers and manufacturers out of the business because the law created a mountain of red tape that severely restricted the hemp industry. For example, while the government would issue tax licenses for farmers to grow hemp, it refused to issue the necessary permits to ship it across state lines to processing plants. These restrictions continue today as farmers begin a drive to revive the American hemp crop. If they succeed, they'll already be behind the dozens of other nations that already permit hemp cultivation, including France, Germany, Canada, and England.

The title shot to the government's cinematic tribute to hemp.

Hemp for Victory

The U.S. hemp industry temporarily revived during World War II. That's when military necessity overcame political concerns about the association between hemp and marijuana. The war had cut off the supply of hemp from the Philippines and India, creating shortages at home. So the government launched a campaign to encourage American farmers to once again grow hemp. Called "Hemp for Victory," the effort included generous government hemp subsidies and a massive educational campaign instructing farmers on the best ways to grow it.

A short *Hemp for Victory* film was part of the government's patriotic plea to farmers. The film was remarkably complimentary of a plant that had just been denounced by the same government's drug officials as the evil weed. The narrator praises its long service to mankind, and to Americans in particular, pointing out how pioneers once rode in Conestoga wagons covered in hemp canvas. U.S. drug officials had blackened the image of marijuana by linking it to words such as "amok" and "assassin." For the more socially acceptable hemp, the government went the other way, pointing out the more benevolent connection between "canvas" and the hemp plant's botanical name, "cannabis."

> **The government launched a campaign to encourage American farmers to once again grow hemp.**

Despite the film's upbeat music and patriotic themes, hemp was a hard sell.

U.S. Army hemp supplies.

The film glosses over the bureaucratic quagmire set up by the Marijuana Tax Act, briefly reminding farmers that there was this little matter of a tax license they would have to buy before they could even plant hemp seeds. The film's "whistle-while-you-work" score merrily chirps away in the background, contrasting sharply with the bleak images of the grueling hemp harvest and processing. Farmers are seen hacking away by hand at unwieldy stands of hemp, and stooping over to flip hemp sheaths that are retting on the ground. Farmers had to take heed at every stage of hemp cultivation, the narrator warned, making sure they planted seeds at the proper distance from each other, while taking care not to overlap hemp sheaths during harvesting, which would make the job even harder. Machines were available to aid the cause, but the circumstances had to be just right. Farmers were told that a pickup binder would work only if the hemp wasn't tangled, but keeping it apart was no easy task.

In 1942, U.S. farmers produced fourteen thousand acres of hemp. The goal for the following year was a whopping increase to three hundred thousand. However, despite urging farmers to grow hemp, the U.S. government soon undercut those efforts by scaling back its hemp subsidy program in 1944. Military agencies refused to buy hemp at inflated prices. Hemp straw began piling up at government mills. Near the war's end, low-priced foreign imports of substitute fibers such as sisal and jute began arriving from Central America. American farmers protested the cutbacks into the hemp market, not wishing to see their subsidies disappear. They had anticipated that the government would continue to prop up the hemp market long after the war had ended. But it never happened. Domestic hemp production declined, and soon after the war, it was once again a forgotten crop.

One person pushing for a strong U.S. hemp industry was Henry Ford, although he was overcome by market forces. He researched the creation of hemp fuels in the 1930s. He also created cheap but resilient plastics from hemp. Ford was such a strong hemp backer that he supervised the building of a car made of a combination of hemp and soybeans. The 1941 model was designed to run on hemp fuel. In this photo, Ford himself demonstrates the hemp car's toughness for the media by gleefully attacking it with a large club.

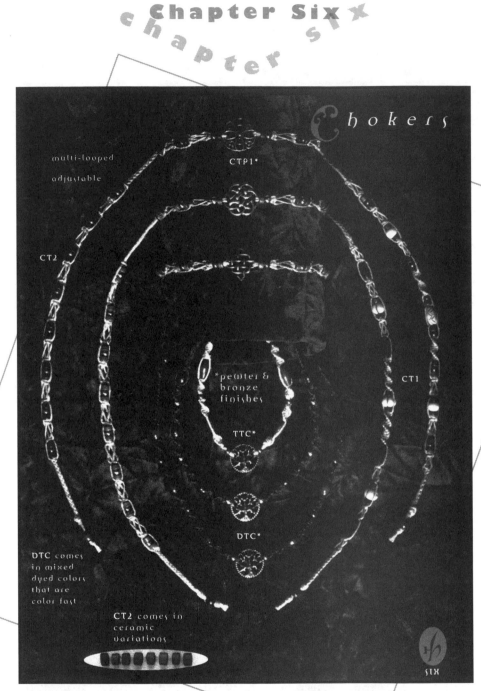

Chokers

multi-looped

adjustable

CTP1*

CT2

*pewter &
bronze
finishes

CT1

TTC*

DTC*

DTC comes
in mixed
dyed colors
that are
color fast

CT2 comes in
ceramic
variations

SIX

Harvest House, the first 100% hemp jewelry retail and wholesale company in the country,
has been creating hemp accessories, such as these, since 1989.

windwise woman
facing south
wisdom whisping
waves of rays
around her shores

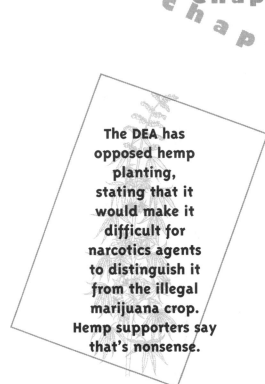

The DEA has opposed hemp planting, stating that it would make it difficult for narcotics agents to distinguish it from the illegal marijuana crop. Hemp supporters say that's nonsense.

The New Hemp Market

As the hemp market has experienced a revival, America has seen its hemp imports increase rapidly, jumping 400% from 1995 to 1996. Much of this hemp is coming from Turkey, El Salvador, and Hungary. The resurgence is being fueled by a dizzying array of hemp products, and one that continues to grow as brand-name makers have climbed aboard the hemp train. Fashion designer Calvin Klein went out of his way to praise hemp as "the fiber of choice in both the home furnishings and fashion industries."

If the hemp market continues to boom, it will do so without the immediate help of American growers. Like a pesky vine, marijuana keeps strangling hemp's effort to break out. The DEA has opposed hemp planting, stating that it would make it difficult for narcotics agents to distinguish it from the illegal marijuana crop. Hemp supporters say that's nonsense. While marijuana plants are set far apart to encourage the growth of leaves, hemp plants are sown close together to promote better stalks.

Despite its tricky legal status, hemp has other things going for it. Manufacturers are intrigued by its tensile strength. Patagonia, for example, makers of popular outdoor wear, conclude that hemp is at least eight times stronger than other natural fibers.

Seeds of a new industry.

Hemp clothes, once unreliable, are now becoming more refined. Retailers such as The Organic Cotton and Hemp Store's Dean Walker are setting high standards. Before he puts a price tag on any hemp item in his store, Walker and his sales staff test it out. They munch on hemp seed snack items and smear hemp lotions and oils on their bodies. If it's an article of clothing he's considering, watch out.

Dean Walker, owner of the Organic Cotton and Hemp Store, models some of the products he sells in his store.

organic-minded customers. The lotion is dispensed from a plastic-wrapped container—right off, an environmental no-no. And Walker didn't think the concept of an artificial tan would catch on with his customers either.

"I take it home and destroy it. I turn it inside out, I try and pull it apart," Walker points out. "There's a lot of crap out there." He says he only likes about a quarter of what he sees, and he sees quite a lot. He has files on over five hundred manufacturers, and the list keeps growing.

Meanwhile, they keep sending samples, some of which make it onto the store shelves. Walker speaks favorably of one new product, hemp flour, but passes on another, a hemp tanning lotion. He didn't think it would be popular with his more

Patagonia, makers of popular outdoor wear, conclude that hemp is at least eight times stronger than other natural fibers.

Walker believes that one of the most intriguing aspects of the hemp movement is that it may be the first time in the clothing industry that a fashion trend is being started from the bottom up. Normally, he says, top-name manufacturers set the trends, and then smaller companies "knock off" these styles at lower prices. Hemp clothing, however, is being shaped by undercapitalized start-up companies, some literally run out of garages. "What

we've done is create an industry," Walker states. "So it's moved slower. It's had its problems."

Even if growing were declared legal, hemp cultivation and the hemp products industry would still face an uphill battle. Cultivation techniques have been forgotten, a quality seed bank is lacking, and machinery for processing has to be developed.

156

But everyone keeps trying. Some of the most daring hemp innovators are chefs and brew-masters. Hemp ales are being cracked open at bars from coast to coast. "We're just making beer, that's all," contends a representative for the makers of Hemp Cream Ale, one of several microbrewers mixing hemp seeds with hops. University of California at Berkeley graduate Steve Nordahl, brewmaster at the Frederick Brewing Company in Maryland, adds hemp to his ale while praising its "distinctive nutty character." He's referring to its taste. The ale's marketing slogan is, "It's perfectly legal."

Pure Hemp Paper is guiding us toward the resurgence of hemp. Historically speaking, hemp paper was the rolling paper of choice.

Hemp is slipping into entrees as well as ales. The Galaxy restaurant in Manhattan serves up exotic menu items such as crusted cod with cajun-spiced, ground hemp seed, hemp vinaigrette, and pies made with hemp crust. At the

A new twist on an old snack!

Laughing Planet in Bloomington, Indiana, hemp cheese is a conversation piece. The restaurant is having fun with its advertising, using Cheech and Chong impersonators to comment on how you don't smoke the cheese, you eat it—and it's good for you, too. The restaurant opened during a marijuana crackdown in the college community, but they went ahead with their plans anyway.

A Canadian company has found a niche with treats loaded with hemp seeds and sweetened with honey and brown sugar. There is even a hemp pretzel called the Hempzel, promoted as a highly nutritional snack loaded with proteins and essential oils. At a Hawaiian restaurant, owner Mark Ellman says he adds hemp to his menu because "it's a little bit taboo." Ellman's Avalon eatery offers hemp-crusted pink snapper.

The hemp industry sparked the emergence of glossy trade publications that add a sense of relevancy to the movement, and a stylish "we're legit" statement. Catalogs for the industry have grown more sophisticated, assuming an L.L. Bean sensibility. They show hip, sexy models posed in the countryside, laughing and enjoying life, all the while outfitted in hemp clothing. It makes the hemp industry seem upbeat and hopeful about the future. *Hemp Times* profiles hemp entrepreneurs in glowing terms, acting as a cheering section for the whole industry. While Bob Marley sang about legalizing marijuana, daughters Sharon and Cedella appear in *Hemp Times* smiling and talking up the virtues of hemp.

Hemp museums have opened up to promote the hemp market in Germany, England, and Holland. They've been educating the public about how valuable it is as a fiber. Meanwhile, hemp is also widely promoted on the Internet.

While hemp promoters go out of their way to explain to customers that their

products have virtually no THC in them, still often they are greeted with snickers. There are signs, however, that hemp products are causing problems for some people by triggering positive tests for marijuana. Preliminary research indicates that hemp foods may be broken down into the same metabolites that produce a positive urine drug test for marijuana. A U.S. Air Force sergeant was court-martialed because of a positive marijuana test, but he eventually proved in court that he had been using hemp oil on his skin. Although the relieved sergeant got his military job back, the experience once again pointed out the stigma of hemp being associated with marijuana. While hemp may be good for marijuana, marijuana isn't good for hemp.

Herb and Al
Good ol' friends
otherwise known as
marijuana and alcohol

marijuana in popular culture

reefer madness

As a dynamic plant with widespread influence, marijuana has taken root in many cultural endeavors throughout history. Artists as diverse as an ancient Greek poet and modern-day rappers have turned to marijuana as subject matter. Sometimes they've aimed for the obvious—comedians have had a field day poking fun at the mental lapses and intense food cravings of pot smokers. Other artists are more subtle, as writer Chester Himes was with "Marijuana and a Pistol," a riveting 1940 short story that gets inside the head of

Fitz Ludlow's *The Hasheesh Eater* is one of a handful of often sensational first-person accounts published during this period that introduced lay people to the mysteries of marijuana and hash use.

a two-bit criminal on a marijuana jag.

Marijuana's cultural reach, initially limited to scattered references throughout literature, has greatly expanded as the plant has grown in popularity as a recreational drug. Marijuana has been a supporting and major player in TV shows, films, songs, comedy acts, and literature. Taken as a whole, as they are here, these cultural references illustrate the wide-ranging spectrum of public opinion when it comes to the always controversial plant.

159

Fitz Ludlow, the Hunter S. Thompson
of his day.

widely read by a curious public largely ignorant of the drug's mind-altering ways. Ludlow's *The Hasheesh Eater*, published in 1857 as a magazine article and then a book, is one of a handful of often sensational first-person accounts appearing during this period that introduced lay people to the mysteries of marijuana and hash use.

In Ludlow's work, he describes gradually increasing the hash doses until he catches a tremendous buzz: "I dwelt in a marvelous inner world," he writes. "I existed by turns in different places and various states of being. Now I swept my gondola through the moonlit lagoons of Venice. Now Alp on Alp towered above my view, and the glory of the coming sun flashed purple light upon the topmost icy

Literature

In 1856, Fitz Ludlow, the son of a minister, visited his friend's Poughkeepsie pharmacy. "Have you seen my new acquisitions?" his friend inquired. Drawn closer to a shelf of vials, Ludlow spotted a curious potion. "What is this," he wondered, "*cannabis indica*?"

Ludlow soon discovered that he had found hashish. Intrigued, Ludlow began experimenting with it, much like his college peers would do a century later. More importantly, Ludlow wrote an essay about his experiences with hash that was

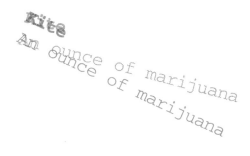

Kite
An ounce of marijuana
An ounce of marijuana

Bill Murray as Hunter S. Thompson and Peter Boyle as his faithful companion Lazlow in *Where the Buffalo Roam*.

latter-day Dr. Gonzo has never found his way back to the main road.

Well before gonzo journalism, there were scattered references to marijuana and hash in historic literature. Homer's *The Odyssey* contains a reference to a drug used by Helen, daughter of Zeus, that sounds like it could have been a hemp drug brought by her from Egypt. Homer calls it "nepenthe," and it is described as a "drug to lull all pain and anger, and to bring forgetfulness of every sorrow." Maybe it

pinnacle." But soon things turned nasty for poor Fitz. He ends his hash trip, so promising at first, on a bummer note: "Hasheesh is indeed an accursed drug, and the soul at last pays a most bitter price for all its ecstasies."

In a way, Fitz Ludlow was the Hunter S. Thompson of his day, placing himself at the vortex of an important journalistic event, albeit with impaired mental function. The difference is that Ludlow's fear and loathing turns him away from drug adventures and toward a career as a high school teacher. Meanwhile, the

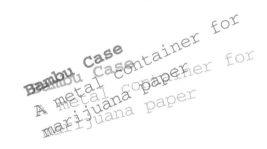

Bambu Case
A metal container for marijuana paper

was poetic license, but Homer describes the drug as being able to ease even the most acute sadness: "whoso should drink a draught thereof . . . would let no tear fall down his cheek, not though his mother and his father died, not though men slew his brother or dear son before his face and his own eyes beheld it."

Two tales from *The Arabian Nights* that include hash references are interesting to mention because they emanate from a culture more tolerant and familiar with hash use. In "The Tale of the Hashish Eater" and "The Tale of Two Hashish Eaters," characters use hash to escape into a fantasy of a better life. One poor man, for example, eats hashish and imagines "a great lord was shampooing him." In the second story, a fisherman and a religious leader swallow enough hashish "to destroy a hundred-year-old elephant." They end up dancing in the street where they meet the Sultan. Like some ancient Cheech and Chong team, they mock him by declaring themselves Sultan. An amused Sultan, respecting the dream-inducing power of the drug, invites them to his palace to remain as storytellers.

Early Gonzos

About the time Fitz Ludlow was tripping on hash tincture in nineteenth-century New York, Theophile Gautier was looking for kicks in Paris at a Left Bank hotel. Gautier was part of a gathering of writers and other cultural elites known as the Club des Haschischins. The group's drug-induced bacchanals drew the likes of Victor Hugo, Alexandre Dumas, Eugene Delacroix, and others. Gautier wrote about his experiences, describing how guests were routinely given a morsel of greenish hash paste upon arrival at the hotel.

Oh, those memorable Arabian Nights...

Gautier recalled one evening when an elegant meal was served on fine china as the guests—including the author—began feeling the effects of the drug.

"The water I drank seemed the most exquisite wine, the meat, once in my mouth, became strawberries, the strawberries, meat," Gautier writes. But then things turned decidedly less pleasant. "A deadening warmth pervaded my limbs, and dementia, like a wave which breaks foaming onto a rock, then withdraws to break again, invaded and left my brain, finally enveloping it altogether." Gautier's reactions are so intense that some scholars suggest he was consuming drugs much stronger than hash at these gatherings.

Another hash club member who recorded his experiences was Charles Baudelaire, who published essays titled "The Seraphic Theatre" and "The Poem of Hashish." Baudelaire praises the "superior sharpness" of his senses and the acute appreciation of music while he's high, but he is ultimately critical of how the plant's recreational use might undermine society's moral structure.

Honore de Balzac also attended the hash club gatherings, but probably didn't indulge in the eating of the special paste. Dumas is another story. He wrote about hash in the novel *The Count of Monte Cristo*. The narrator encounters a stranger on a desert island named Sinbad, who serves him a feast that includes a "greenish paste." He's told the paste will open up a sumptuous dream world.

Writer Gustav Flaubert experimented with hash, and at the time of his death was outlining a novel based on a character who goes insane from the drug.

Chapter seven

Writer Gustav Flaubert experimented with hash, and at the time of his death was outlining a novel based on a character who goes insane from the drug. More surprising is the dominance of hash in Louisa May Alcott's *Perilous Play* of 1869. In this story, bored characters searching for "a new and interesting amusement" partake of some hashish: "'Oh yes. It's that Indian stuff which brings one fantastic visions, isn't it?'" one character exclaims. Soon they fall under its spell, and Alcott's description of the stoned gathering could stand for pot parties of later generations: "Belle laughed often, a silvery ringing laugh, pleasant to hear; but when complimented on her good spirits, she looked distressed and said she could not help her merriment; Meredith was quite calm but rather dreamy; Evelyn was pale and her next neighbor heard her heart beat; Norton talked incessantly..." Nothing extraordinary or harmful happens in the story, although characters fret about impending disaster throughout.

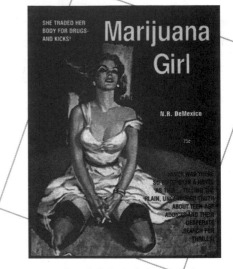

When she's bad, she's very bad.

Many mass market paperbacks from this time featured lurid covers and titillating cover copy with the goal of enticing readers to fork over a quarter to buy them.

Modern Marijuana Literature

Modern writers have woven marijuana into their work in a variety of ways, reflecting society's growing sophistication with the plant as a recreational drug. A short and poignant use of marijuana in hard-boiled fiction is "Marijuana and a Pistol," a taut short story by Chester Himes. Petty criminal Red Caldwell, upset over losing his girl,

10¢ WILLIAM IRISH

A cheap and evil girl sets a hopped-up killer against a city.

MARIHUANA

COMPLETE AND UNABRIDGED

The marijuana menace as pulp fiction.

experience the disjointed thoughts and confused state of a person who is high on marijuana.

In stark contrast to this subtle tale are several pulp fiction novels from the 1940s and 1950s that targeted marijuana use in sensational ways. Many mass market paperbacks from this time featured lurid covers and titillating cover copy with the goal of enticing readers to fork over a quarter to buy them. Any type of moral degradation was fair game for subject matter, so marijuana, controversial and the target of a hysteria campaign, made for juicy pulp fiction drama.

Marihuana, by William Irish, features cover art of a supine woman in a slinky red dress with the sinister green face of a leering man perched over her. A smoking reefer practically covers her torso due to the unusual perspective of the art. The cover copy reads: "A cheap and evil girl sets a hopped-up killer against a city."

Marijuana Girl combines two pulp fiction favorites—drug abuse and loose women. On its cover, a reefer-smoking redhead in a sexy slip dreamily stares ahead, apparently, as the copy says, having just

brings a .38 revolver and two "weeds" into his room. Once he smokes the reefers, his fate is sealed. In a dream-like trance he embarks on a brief but deadly crime spree, unaware of what he's done. It may be one of the first pieces of fiction to get inside the head of a reefer smoker in a realistic way. The effect of reading the story is to

165

Chapter sev

Allen Ginsburg, Timothy Leary, and Ralph Metzner: High Priests of the Beat Generation.

"traded her body for drugs and kicks!" Like many pulp fiction works, the actual novels were far more tame than the covers suggested.

One group of modern writers clearly associated with marijuana are "the Beats." Jack Kerouac talked about writing as if he were "blowing" jazz, so it's no surprise that he did what many jazz players have done—he got high to pursue his art. Pot plays a role in the debauchery at a Mexican whorehouse in Kerouac's *On the Road.* Beat poets probably smoked as much grass as their musical predecessors, jazz vipers.

In 1965, Allen Ginsberg expressed his views on marijuana with an essay entitled "The First Manifesto to End the Bringdown." He wrote half of it while high, widely praising this mental state for its ability to transform the way he looked at the world. He recalls the pleasures of visiting New York City museums while stoned and suddenly appreciating the works of artists such as Klee and Cezanne. "I apprehend the structure of certain pieces of jazz and classic music in a new manner under the influence of marijuana, and these apprehensions have remained in the years of normal consciousness," Ginsberg writes. This is not an idle pot head, but one of America's greatest writers offering an eloquent treatise on the joys of getting high.

The fictional equivalent of Ginsberg's essay is Terry Southern's "Red-Dirt Marijuana." Southern is a satirical author who also wrote *Candy* and *The Magic Christian*. Southern's short marijuana story is mostly a conversation between a young white boy, Harold, and an older black farm hand named C.K., who teaches him all about the joys of "gage." When Harold finds some wild gage and brings it to C.K., the farm hand immediately tries to interest the boy in smoking some, telling him it will make him feel as good as when he got his new Winchester rifle at Christmas. He explains the subtleties from cleaning it to the different levels of potency, but Harold remains skeptical, wanting to know why marijuana is illegal if it's so good. Southern's story creates a very sympathetic character in the gage-loving C.K., and also offers several provocative arguments in favor of making marijuana legal.

One modern writer whose pot themes can't be ignored is Thomas Pynchon, who was "outed" as a major pot head in a 1977 article by Jules Siegel in *Playboy* magazine. Siegel relates several encounters of getting stoned with the author, and even quotes him as saying that he was "fucked up" when he was writing a first draft of *Gravity's Rainbow*, which won the National Book Award in 1974. Could it be that Pynchon's themes of paranoia are pot-induced? Check out Pynchon's *Vineland*, in which the pot-growing region of Northern California is under siege by sinister DEA agents. The novel is woven with labyrinthine subplots and conspiracy theories.

Imagining Pynchon as some cloistered stoner makes it easier to understand the scene he created of a U.S. president who does inhale. In a wildly hilarious passage in *Mason & Dixon*, the two surveyors referred to in the title of the book meet up

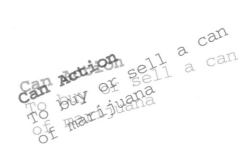

Can Action
To buy or sell a can
of marijuana

One modern writer whose pot themes can't be ignored is Thomas Pynchon, who was "outed" as a major pot head in a 1977 article by Jules Siegel in *Playboy* magazine.

1946, a character named Honey Brown gets high and then robs a store. John Updike, in *Rabbit Redux*, creates a washed-up lounge singer who offers Harry Angstrom a joint and is later busted for marijuana possession. In the *Last of the Red Hot Lovers*, written by Neil Simon in 1969, a hippie character lures others into smoking some pot. Twenty years later, David Rabe scripted a scene in *Hurlyburly* with two characters snorting cocaine and smoking marijuana. This scene is more reflective of the times, showing the characters doing drugs in the natural course of daily life.

with General Washington during the course of their work in America, and he quickly dispatches his slave to gather up the necessary smoking supplies: "'Gershom fetch us if you will some Pipes, and Bowl of the new-cur'd Hemp. And another gallon of your magnificent Punch.'" Very soon Martha appears with a tray of tarts, popovers, fried pies, and doughnuts: "'Smelled that Smoak, figur'd you'd be needing something to nibble on,' the doughty Mrs. W. greets them."

Some modern writers have been less imaginative with pot references, sometimes using them as crude tools to reflect character flaws. In *The Member of the Wedding*, written by Carson McCullers in

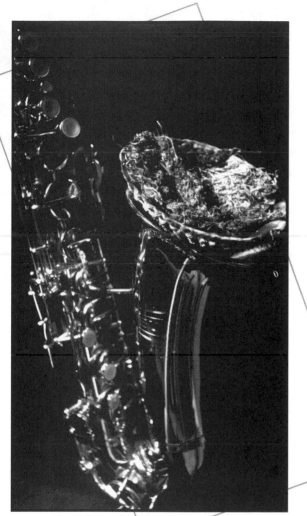

Music

It's no coincidence that the roots of jazz and the rise of marijuana smoking in America can be tied to the same time and place. Both came out of the bordello community of Storyville in New Orleans around 1910. The herb's well-documented effects of slowing down time and increasing sensory awareness has made it a popular sideman for musicians everywhere.

For early jazz players, pot was a revelation. While high, they learned to add slurs, melodic phrases, and syncopation that created an overall "hot" sound. By the early 1940s, the powerful effects of marijuana smoking on jazz musicians was observed in the media. An article in *Time* magazine articulated the phenomenon, with more than a hint of disdain for its alleged boost in playing ability: "The drug's power to slow the sense of time gives the improviser the illusion that he has all the time in the world in which to conceive the next phrase. And the drug also seems to heighten the hearing—so that, for instance, strange chord formations seem easier to analyze under marijuana."

Some jazz musicians began to look down on vipers, the players who needed to get high before they could play "hot." In turn, vipers felt superior to those musicians who drank. Vipers believed alcohol made players sloppier as the evening wore on, and caused greater long-term health consequences. In the song "You Rascal You," a jazz viper taunts the musical lush by pointing out how he would be "standing on the corner high when they bring your body by."

It's no coincidence that the roots of jazz and the rise of marijuana smoking in America can be tied to the same time and place. Both came out of the bordello community of Storyville in New Orleans around 1910.

One of the first people to articulate the role of marijuana in jazz playing was a white Jewish sideman named Milton Mezzrow. Born in Chicago, Mezzrow was playing a club gig in 1923 when he took his first toke during a break. He returned a different player: "The first thing I noticed was that I began to hear my saxophone as though it were inside my head . . . I found I was slurring much better and putting just the right feeling in my phrases—I was really coming on," he wrote. "I began to

feel very happy and sure of myself." In 1946, he published his experiences in a book titled *Really the Blues*. While Mezzrow never distinguished himself as a player, he became legendary for the quality of the pot he sold to fellow musicians. His stuff was so good that the word "Mezz" became synonymous with potent smoke.

Candy Jag
To crave sweets after smoking marijuana

Cab Calloway immortalized "The Reefer Man." Hi-De-Ho!

Jazz songs celebrating the joys of reefer began surfacing by the 1930s, including Cab Calloway's "The Reefer Man" of 1932, which immortalized that "funny reefer man" who "walks the ocean every time he gets the notion." Other jazz tunes of the era include "If You're a Viper," "Save the Roach for Me" and "The Stuff Is Here."

171

sang about his preference for "muggles," slang for joints. Armstrong was arrested for pot as early as 1931, and would later tell biographers,"Well, that was life and I don't feel ashamed. Mary Warner, honey, you sure was good."

A list of jazz players who dabbled in marijuana would run as long as a Charlie Parker bebop phrase. That fact didn't escape Bureau of Narcotics Commissioner Harry Anslinger. He ordered agents to keep tabs on well-known jazz musicians such as Parker, Armstrong, Thelonious Monk, Count Basie, Duke Ellington, Cab Calloway, and even orchestras for NBC, the Milton Berle Show, and the Jackie Gleason Show.

Vipers didn't just exist in smoky clubs either. In 1944, a drummer for the NBC orchestra was arrested at NBC studios in New York City for literally smoking in the boy's room. Anslinger linked marijuana and such "hot" styles of jazz as swing with the moral decay of America's youth. Testifying before a Senate Committee,

Louis Armstrong, a lifelong smoker, sang about his preference for "muggles," slang for joints. Armstrong was arrested for pot as early as 1931, and would later tell biographers, "Well, that was life and I don't feel ashamed. Mary Warner, honey, you sure was good."

Charlie Parker

Harry Anslinger ordered his agents to keep tabs on such well-known jazz musicians as Charlie Parker, Duke Ellington, Thelonius Monk, Louis Armstrong, Count Basie...even the orchestras for the Milton Berle and Jackie Gleason shows. Being a jazz musician automatically made government drug agents suspicious.

Duke Ellington

Marijuana was always in the air at a Grateful Dead show.

Dylan declared that "Everybody Must Get Stoned!"

Anslinger identified musicians as repeat offenders of marijuana laws. "And I don't mean good musicians. I mean jazz musicians," he added with scorn. The viper problem percolated to the pages of *Down Beat* magazine in 1943 in an article admonishing pot-toking musicians to "stop it now before you get yourself and friends in a potfull of trouble."

Despite legal restrictions and other warnings about pot dangers, marijuana continues to play a role in jazz music and has branched out to every musical genre. A century that dawned with pot-smoking jazz vipers in New Orleans ended with marijuana being trumpeted by musical artists playing styles as diverse as country and heavy metal. The habit not only became popular with musicians but also their audiences. The sweet aroma of ganja, once confined to smoky jazz clubs, began wafting through 1950's coffeehouses, and a decade later at outdoor rock concerts.

The Grateful Dead's hypnotic concert improvisations were ideally suited to being under the influence of something, especially great sinsemilla. Artists during the 1960s and 1970s singing about getting stoned included Bob Dylan, who decreed that "everybody must get stoned" in "Rainy Day Women #12 & 35." Steve Miller's "The Joker" was a midnight-toking kind of guy. Sly Stone told us "I want to take you higher." Other notable rock songs about marijuana include Black Sabbath's "Sweet Leaf," Steppenwolf's "Don't Step on the Grass, Sam," and Neil Young's "Homegrown," among many others too numerous to mention.

Blues and country have long had their marijuana followers. Blues singer Muddy Waters wailed on about his "champagne and reefer." Pot advocate and country singer Willie Nelson went right from jail on a pot bust to the music studio to record a duet with Frank Sinatra in 1994. Nelson also

Nelson. Willie, that is.

> **Pot advocate and country singer Willie Nelson went right from jail on a pot bust to the music studio to record a duet with Frank Sinatra in 1994. Nelson also claims to have toked up in the White House during the Carter administration.**

claims to have toked up in the White House during the Carter administration.

The musical genre most closely associated with marijuana is reggae, in large part due to two prominent artists: Bob Marley and Peter Tosh. The caricature of the dreadlocked Rastafarian wouldn't be complete without a smoking joint. In 1976, Marley's "Rastaman Vibration" included a liner reference that spelled out what every pot head already knew: "This album jacket is great for cleaning herb." That same year, Tosh came out with what would become a pro-pot anthem, "Legalize It." Marley was quoted in one interview explaining why he thought many people felt threatened by ganja smoking: "System don't agree with herb because herb make ya too solid."

Pro-pot musicians eventually became more outspoken about their love of the herb. Rapper Dr. Dre's *The Chronic*, slang for a powerful strain of pot, was a high-profile example of this trend. The album included a cover bearing the declaration, "In Bud We Trust." The heavy metal band Guns N' Roses and Southern rockers the Black Crowes were pro-pot in lyrics and spirit, with the latter band sometimes performing against the backdrop of a colossal marijuana leaf.

Dre gets Chronic.

Marley was quoted in one interview explaining why he thought many people felt threatened by ganja smoking: "System don't agree with herb because herb make ya too solid."

Cypress Hill climbed to the top of this trend with their *Black Sunday* album that included "I Wanna Get High" and "Hits from the Bong"; that the album sold a quarter-million copies in its first week of release was one of many factors signaling trouble to anti-drug forces. Not only did a hit pot song mean that youths would be listening to pro-drug lyrics, they would also be seeing pro-pot images on music videos. The videos, in turn, promoted a fashion craze in pot-themed outfits. Cypress Hill's B-Real, who began doing media interviews while toking on an electric bong, touted pot not only for its pleasurable smoke but also as a valuable fiber. One of his favorite refrains was "Legalizing marijuana could bring a lot of American jobs back."

NORML's tribute to hemp featured such bands as The Black Crowes and Blues Traveler.

Musical Censors

With much of the music industry controlled by large, conservative companies, it wasn't long before the smoke hit the fan for pro-marijuana musicians. Disney officials reportedly weren't happy when one of its heavy metal artists, Sacred Reich, called attention to its *Independent* album by sending along bongs with promotional material. Jamiroquai singer Jay K was forced to change the lyrics of his hit "Return of the Space Cowboy" for a music video. In the video, "cheeba," which is slang for marijuana, was changed to "Freeba," while the lyric "gotta get high" was altered to "gotta get sly."

To show the absurdity of some of these attempts at censorship, the Japanese trio Shonen Knife ran into problems with the seemingly innocent song "Catnip Dream." The song describes how catnip makes cats feel dreamy. The song's author, bass player Michie Nakatani, tried to explain that there were no hidden meanings to the tune.

Bernie Brightman

TEA PAD SONGS VOLUME ONE

*TEA PAD — A PLACE WHERE MARIJUANA IS SMOKED

Bernard Brightman was a kid from Brooklyn venturing into 1930's Harlem for an evening of dancing when he discovered marijuana smoking. He was on his way with friends to the Savoy Ballroom, the "Home of Happy Feet." They were drinking a little, of course. Then they met an acquaintance who suggested something else. "Why don't you let me get you some reefer?" he offered. "We said, 'Sure. What is it?'" Brightman recalls. After forking over a quarter for

Bernie Brightman, 1938.

three reefer cigarettes, they soon found out. "We got stoned out of our heads. We were very happy," Brightman remembers.

That was Brightman's introduction to marijuana and the world of jazz vipers—marijuana-toking musicians who frequented popular nightspots in Harlem in the 1930s and 1940s. "Marijuana culture was mainly among jazz people, carnival people, and the black population who were close to jazz in urban areas such as New Orleans, New York, and Chicago," Brightman points out. "It was mostly the outsiders of society."

Marijuana was a key part of an inexpensive evening of entertainment for Brightman and his friends. They rode a train for 5 cents to Harlem and then paid 20 cents to get into places like the Savoy for an evening of great music and dancing. "You could smoke in the bathroom with impunity. It also broke down racial barriers. You'd get to meet the musicians there on a friendly

basis—they were smoking too. It was a real friendly atmosphere, until the laws changed."

With marijuana prohibition in 1937, smokers became more discreet, stepping into telephone booths or crawling under tables to light up. Brightman says he bought regularly from two reefer men—Crappy and Mickey—who sold it openly on a street corner, and later opened a candy store on the same spot. Brightman and his reefer friends eventually bought in bulk. They could score an ounce for $8. They would buy special rolling papers from a Spanish grocery store, and then rent a hotel room for $1, where they would roll up their entire stash.

Brightman remembers hanging out in "tea pads" around Harlem during this period, too. These were informal gathering spots where reefer heads could smoke and enjoy each other's company. "Tea pads were so sexual," Brightman observes. "The lights were low, and there was good grass and music."

A four-year stint in the Air Force during World War II didn't dampen Brightman's

Chapter seven

marijuana habit. Because the U.S. government was growing it as part of the war effort, Brightman says marijuana was easy to find. Military tokers would ask each other if they were "sticking," which meant they had some reefer. They would mail it to each other to make sure everyone was adequately supplied.

After the war, Brightman toned down his marijuana smoking for extended periods when he worked in the family business selling handbags and when he became involved in political causes, such as the Communist Party. For a while he sold hash after buying a massive quantity of it without even knowing what hash was. "It was so fantastic," Brightman recollects with obvious pleasure. "One toke was sufficient to get you stoned. People were buying aspirin cans and making water pipes and smoking it that way.

They were selling tokes at Coney Island for 50 cents. It was pretty crazy, pretty wild."With such fond memories, it's no wonder that Brightman founded a record label in 1975 that pays tribute to vintage reefer songs of the 1930s and 1940s. Released under labels such as Stash and

Viper's Nest, Brightman's compilations of reefer songs and other obscure blues and jazz music revived classic marijuana tunes at a time when the drug was experiencing an upsurge in popularity. Some of the tunes feature well-known musicians, including Ella Fitzgerald, Cab Calloway, Champion Jack Dupree, Fats Waller, and Gene Krupa. They also offer some of the colorful lingo that permeated marijuana culture at the time, reflected in song titles such as "Killin' Jive," "A Viper's Moan," "Reefer Song," and "The 'G' Man got the 'T' Man."

For Brightman, musical testimonials to marijuana are fitting, because they celebrate a drug he found enjoyable. "Marijuana was much better than drinking liquor and getting drunk. And it enhanced a lot of things for me, from sex to music and food. It enhanced a lot of things which are pleasurable. And if you were open to change, it could change your consciousness for certain."

The kings of pot comedy.

Pot in Film

Pot heads have never fared well in the movies. In early scare films, reefer heads were portrayed as losing their minds as the first wisps of smoke entered their lungs. Marijuana made them instant lunatics. In horror movies, lighting up a joint was an open invitation for killers to make the unfortunate character their next victim. This formula was played out in countless teen slasher flicks. As soon as a young couple drifts into the woods to smoke a joint and have sex, they're as good as dead. In the horror film *The Relic*, a guard at a museum sneaks into a bathroom for a few puffs on a joint while on his rounds. Before he can savor his high, he's behead-ed by an evil beast. Coming upon the mur-der scene, a cop comments, "Pot's a mis-demeanor. Decapitation seems a bit severe."

The tone for marijuana in film was set during the 1930s. This decade featured three notable movies designed to shock

Lila gets wild.

These movies show audiences how marijuana turns chaste women into flirtatious hussies and, in some cases, homicidal maniacs. Each of these films begins with a stern-faced narrator highlighting the seriousness of the problem. Of course, the narrator doesn't want to have to show audiences the following shocking scenes. But this titillating entertainment is necessary to educate them, the narrator explains.

The government clamped down on drug films after passage of the Marijuana Tax Act of 1937. Directors rarely attempted them during the 1940s, but an exception

audiences and rouse them into action against the marijuana menace. The bias is in their titles: *Assassin of Youth*, *Reefer Madness*, and *Marihuana: The Weed with Roots in Hell*. These movies seem ludicrous today because of their overstatement and crude acting. In *Reefer Madness*, smokers inhale one puff and their eyes bug out and they laugh hysterically, as if they've become instant idiots. One youthful convert to reefers wildly drives his car over a pedestrian without realizing what he's done. In *Assassin*, a man sits catatonic on a couch. When asked to show another guest where he might score some reefer, he points to a blank wall behind him and says, "See that fellow behind me? Get some from him."

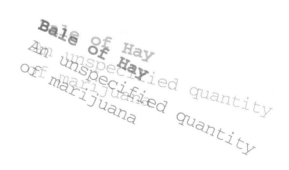

Bale of Hay
An unspecified quantity of marijuana

was *Wild Weed*, which starred Lila Leeds. She was an actress busted with Robert Mitchum for pot smoking. While Mitchum's career got right back on track after his release from prison, Leeds didn't do as well. She was relegated to B-movie roles after her bust. *Wild Weed* harkens back to earlier scare films. It includes a scene of a stoned piano player clumsily banging away at the piano while imagining himself giving a concert recital, and a reefer head who tokes up and then screams, "I know I'm going to die!"

In *Reefer Madness*, smokers inhale one puff and their eyes bug out and they laugh hysterically, as if they've become instant idiots. One youthful convert to reefers wildly drives his car over a pedestrian without realizing what he's done.

The emergence of anti-heroes in the 1950s brought drugs and other illegal behavior back to the big screen, most notably in films such as *High School Confidential* in 1958. In this supercharged high school drama, Russ Tamblyn plays a jive-talking school tough who transfers to a new school and looks to make an immediate impact as the main drug dealer on campus. The film draws a line between weed use and harder drugs, implying that marijuana wasn't as dangerous.

Echoing earlier scare films, *High School Confidential* inserts a lecture by a police commissioner, who warns school officials about the evils of marijuana. The difference here is that this lecture is now woven into the story line. When a teacher expresses doubts about the cop's dire predictions, he counters with a story of a school in Indiana where they didn't think they had a problem either. But then a 13-year-old marijuana addict ended up dead, he says. Even with the horrible story, school officials remain skeptical, certainly a reflection of how society was beginning to doubt some of the overstated dangers of marijuana smoking.

One other notable 1950's movie involving marijuana is *Touch of Evil*, Orson Welles's

Jack and Peter toke it up around the campfire in *Easy Rider.*

sordid tale of a murder investigation in a Mexican border town. Welles's corrupt American cop tries to frame the wife of Mexican policeman Charlton Heston by having thugs kidnap her and then blow reefer smoke over her clothes in a sleazy hotel room. The thugs leave her naked in bed with reefer "stunts" all around, intending for cops arriving at the scene to assume a wild sex party had transpired.

Just like earlier scare films, it's implied that the reefer could have led Heston's wife, played by Janet Leigh, to become a drug-crazed sex maniac who might even commit murder.

An upswing of marijuana smoking in the 1960s brought more pot images to film, mirroring what was happening in society. For the first time, the evils of marijuana smoking weren't the main focus of a

186

While Bob and Natalie smoke a bowl in *Bob, Carol, Ted, and Alice.*

movie. Still, pot smoking was associated mostly with rebels, hippies, and other counterculture characters. In *Easy Rider*, Jack Nicholson is introduced to pot smoking by Peter Fonda and Dennis Hopper, and it promotes deep thinking on his part—once he masters the art of inhaling.

In *Bob and Carol and Ted and Alice*, smoking pot meshes nicely with the film's free-wheeling sex themes, while in *I Love You, Alice B. Toklas* of 1968, the introduc-

tion of marijuana into the life of the straight lawyer played by Peter Sellers completely changes his view of the world. His spiritual awakening occurs after he accidentally eats pot brownies, along with his parents and fiancée. The brownies turn his parents into laughing maniacs and make his fiancée sexually frisky. "Take me," she pleads with him, as he struggles to get her off him. Sellers' awakening has its consequences, and he later grows weary of his newfound hippie lifestyle.

187

Marijuana turns Peter
Sellars from a buttoned-
down attorney to a
freewheeling hippie in
I Love You, Alice B. Toklas.

Any discussion of pot and film has to include Cheech and Chong. The bungling, lovable stoners, who never learned to say no, set the standard for pot comedy with their stage routines, hit records, and six films. During their 16-year run, which ended in 1987, they targeted their humor at a drug-savvy young audience. They showed the lighter side of getting high—the munchies, the forgetfulness, the stupid excess...Cheech would spend half the film with a blank, squinty-eyed look, as if never sure of what he was seeing. With his trademark headband, spaced-out demeanor, and frequent use of "Far out, man!" Tommy Chong was the pot-head's pot head. He'd pull joints the size of prized cucumbers out of his pocket. He was the clown prince of cannabis, gleefully discovering a tiny roach and lighting it up with joy, only to suck the burning bud down his throat, causing him to scream in pain.

The duo loved mocking justice. In *Up in Smoke*, they smuggle marijuana from Mexico into the United States by driving a van actually made of the stuff. Even with being so obvious, the bungling narcs, led by Stacey Keach, let Cheech and Chong cross the border and instead arrest the wrong suspects—a carload of nuns. This humor reflects the period's more relaxed

Tommy Chong, mayor of Stonerville.

Before long everyone was lighting up, even Jack Lemmon in *Save the Tiger*. In one scene, Lemmon's character is offered some grass and he responds knowingly by saying, "We used to call it gage." Donald Sutherland and Jane Fonda toke up in *Klute* in 1971, while Woody Allen gets a contact high by stepping into a smoke-filled cab just vacated by stoners in *Play it Again, Sam* in 1972.

views toward pot—the perception was that the law would never catch up with stoners.

A more recent comedy film that harkens back to Cheech and Chong is 1997's *Half-Baked*. The film's plot revolves around bungling pot heads planning to deal marijuana in order to raise bail for a friend in jail. The film is pro-marijuana, and includes a seductive scene of the group floating along in the sky while high. When the main character goes to a substance abuse gathering, he's heckled from the room because they

Dazed and Confused.

don't consider pot to be a serious drug problem. This is clearly a film produced by people who know their stuff. One scene has a smoker preparing to make a homemade bong. First, he asks for a toilet paper roll, corkscrew, and tinfoil. Told these aren't available, he replies, "OK, an avocado, ice pick, and snorkel."

The film features cameos by Willie Nelson, Tommy Chong, and Snoop Doggy Dog. When Nelson goes to buy pot from the group and is told how much it costs, he retorts, "Sixty dollars? I remember when a dime bag was a dime."

Despite pot's increasing presence in films, stoners have never really escaped the stereotype of being listless losers. In *Fast Times at Ridgemont High*, Sean Penn's character is a toking slacker, followed a decade later by the youthful underachievers in *Dazed and Confused* and *The Stoned Age*. Serial bonger Bridget Fonda in *Jackie Brown* can

190

barely make it off the couch. The archetyp-al stoner-slacker is Jeff Bridges in *The Big Lebowski*, a man introduced as one of the laziest in the world, and one who at times can barely muster the energy to complete a thought.

One modern film that tells a marijuana story in a realistic manner is Stephen Gyllenhaal's *Homegrown*. Billed as a *Treasure of the Sierra Madre* for dope growers, it's a comedy-drama set in Northern California's famed pot-growing region during harvest time. When three people assigned to guard a remote marijuana patch see their boss killed and the multimillion-dollar crop left behind, they decide to market it themselves. Their paranoia is somewhat brought on by their constant marijuana smoking but is also understandable, since so much money is at stake. The film captures the disparity between the serenity of the scenic region's laid-back community and the undercur-rent of drug violence. A long-time grower played by Jamie Lee Curtis comments, "You

start dealing with the wrong people, bad shit happens, even in a place like this."

Half Baked features cameos by Willie Nelson, Tommy Chong, and Snoop Doggy Dog. When Nelson goes to buy pot from the group and is told how much it costs, he retorts, "Sixty dollars? I remember when a dime bag was a dime."

A slacking toker, or a toker slacking?

Pot and Television

During the early days of television drama, pot heads were almost always on the wrong side of the law. Police shows of the 1960s and 1970s found a popular target in marijuana dealers and users, often lumping them together with pushers of harder drugs, such as heroin and cocaine, and more serious criminals, such as murderers and thieves.

Jack Webb and Harry Morgan on *Dragnet* went after assorted marijuana criminals with their usual dogged style, even once busting an entire family that believed

> **Jack Webb and Harry Morgan on *Dragnet* went after assorted marijuana criminals with their usual dogged style, even once busting an entire family that believed marijuana was good and should be legalized.**

marijuana was good and should be legalized. In one episode, Webb rats out a night-school classmate for pot smoking, not stopping to consider the ethics of his police work. Other television law enforcers, such as Jack Lord's McGarrett on *Hawaii Five-O* and Raymond Burr's *Ironside*, all took aim at pot criminals. Even Angie Dickinson, as *Police Woman*, nabbed a marijuana smuggler in one episode.

Marijuana smokers who aren't portrayed as criminals are harder to find on television. In the 1970's comedy *Mary Hartman, Mary Hartman*, Mary finds a joint belong-ing to her teenage daughter. She

"Sgt. Friday, I smell the scent of a marijuana crime."

John Goodman gets friendly with a hookah on *Roseanne*.

The introduction of more risqué programming on cable, as well as some nostalgic programs that explore life in the 1960s and 1970s, have generated more realistic, and less criminal, views of pot use on television. In the HBO comedy *Arliss*, the duplicitous sports agent bonds with a baseball pitcher when he prevents him from getting ripped off during a pot deal. Later, in a fairly natural setting, they share a joint, toking up and talking about their future together. For a little bit of comedy, soon after they get high, Arliss's assistant has an attack of the munchies and demands to know where he can find the nearest White Castle hamburger stand.

On Showtime's comedy-drama *Rude Awakening*, uptight church ladies are accidentally given pot brownies at a baby shower. They end up laughing hysterically, crawling on the furniture and staring blankly at a Jesus mobile intended for the baby's amusement. After eating the brownies, two of the women discover that they're gay and begin kissing.

In the Fox television drama *That '70s Show*, which chronicles the life of several teens during the 1970s, marijuana use is not shown directly but overtly hinted at.

confiscates it, but ends up smoking it with her husband before they go to an encounter session. In the 1990s, on the hit comedy series *Roseanne*, Roseanne and her sister discover an old stash of marijuana and smoke it to get high, laughing together in the bathroom and getting the munchies.

193

"without it I could, uh, go even blinder." In an episode of *Nash Bridges*, Tommy Chong reunites with Cheech Marin by playing a character leading Cheech to a murder suspect at a cannabis club. Chong tells a disbelieving Cheech that under Prop. 215, marijuana is perfectly legal. On *Murphy Brown*, Murphy smokes pot to combat the nausea from chemotherapy. "I'm not only feeling better," she comments, "I'm feeling hungry."

The introduction of more risqué programming on cable, as well as some nostalgic programs that explore life in the 1960s and 1970s, have generated more realistic, and less criminal, views of pot use on television.

The main characters have been shown in the basement, where they sit around talking in a stoned manner. However, no direct smoking is ever portrayed.

Other television shows have examined the medical marijuana issue. In an episode of *The Simpsons*, Bart comes across a blind man at the police station. When Bart's dog knocks a bag of weed from the blind man's pocket in the presence of a deputy, the cop suggests that maybe this could be a case of medical marijuana. "Oh yeah," the blind man says, sensing a way of out trouble,

Cola
The flowering tops of a marijuana plant

Pot and Comedy

George Carlin back in his hippie-dippie weatherman days.

Pot humor can be an easy target. A lot of humor capitalizes on the clichéd side effect of the munchies. For example, Jay Leno stepped into the medical marijuana issue by noting that one of the cannabis clubs in California was looking for a pot dealer. Leno suggested applicants prove their worth by showing up at the interview covered with Cheetos dust. In Drew Carey's standup routine, he mocks pot smokers by saying that marijuana would probably be legal by now if users weren't so stoned that they always forget to vote.

Other comics have spoken out for pot. Bill Maher has told audiences that god made drugs such as marijuana and mushrooms to ease human suffering. "I mean, we have one species of mushrooms that is perfect for a cream sauce, and there's one that makes you laugh for eight straight hours. That doesn't seem random to me," Maher observes. Satirist Paul Krassner took a pro-pot stance by appearing as a special guest at the Cannabis Cup in Amsterdam. Meanwhile, political comedian Rick Overton described for pot lovers the initial rush of buying his first buds in Amsterdam's relaxed environment. "I smelled it. Then I just held it and I started crying, like Miss America, holding it like a bouquet." Finally, comedian George Carlin has told reporters that he occasionally smokes pot to polish up his comedy writing. "I just see and hear things differently," Carlin states.

Chapter Seven

Pot and the Comics

As pot became popular during the 1960s, it became the subject of several underground comic strips. These cartoons were often racy and mocking of many social conventions, so marijuana was an obvious topic. One notable artist who dealt with marijuana was Gilbert Shelton, creator of the "The Fabulous Furry Freak Brothers." The brothers were lovable hippie lowlifes often depicted in pursuit of drugs, including marijuana.

In one episode, Fat is sent to "Ripoff Park" to score some grass, but of course he's held up by thugs, who are, in turn, attacked and robbed themselves. By the end, the park is littered with fallen criminals, and Freddy merely collects their weapons and drug supplies and brings

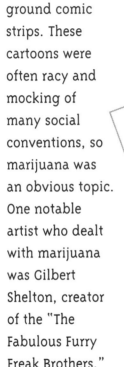

"Killer Grass!"

them home to his brothers. In another Shelton work, he satirizes anti-marijuana hysteria films by drawing one of his own, a panel called "The Truth about the Killer Weed." In the strip, characters fight over a joint, hatch a plan to murder a "little old crippled lady," and then decide to rob a passerby at knifepoint. Everyone ends up dead.

Marijuana has also turned up in mainstream comics and cartoons, including a recent depiction of the medical marijuana issue in the venerable *New Yorker* magazine. In it, a doctor says he can't do much for a patient's condition, but the good news is he can score him some great pot. The widely distributed "Doonesbury" strip by Garry Trudeau has featured the medical marijuana issue, taking a mostly sympathetic view. In one panel, when slacker Zonker Harris first hears about California's proposition to

196

legalize pot for medical use, he turns to a friend and says, "Okay, say I had hay fever …" The pro-stance of the strip angered state Attorney General Dan Lungren, who warned that no one should be laughing. That just made Trudeau a more ardent advocate for the issue in his strip.

Trudeau's bold stance, however, is one not taken by many creators of popular culture. It's certainly not illegal to express views about marijuana through public art and culture, but many people act that way, and for good reason. A pro-marijuana image, in either music, film, TV, or literature, is still not a popular one, and is sure to generate controversy. Pro-marijuana musicians have faced censorship. In other arts, censorship is perhaps self-imposed.

In the 1998 hit comedy film *There's Something About Mary*, the two lead characters sit outside at the end of a long date and share a joint, rather nonchalantly. But these types of everyday depictions of marijuana use are rare in films and other aspects of popular culture. With hysteria films such as *Reefer Madness* now viewed as camp humor, it's obvious that the treatment of marijuana in popular culture has made great strides. But while the

hysteria has faded, common sense has yet to take over.

> **The widely distributed "Doonesbury" strip by Garry Trudeau has featured the medical marijuana issue, taking a mostly sympathetic view. In one panel, when slacker Zonker Harris first hears about California's proposition to legalize pot for medical use, he turns to a friend and says, "Okay, say I had hay fever…"**

Cured
Marijuana soaked in sugar water and then dried

Deck
Pack of marijuana cigarettes

Fall Out
Fall asleep after smoking marijuana

pOt CultUre

"don't bogart that joint, my friend"

When H. H. Kane decided to get stoned in 1885, he didn't have many options. In fact, only one: the local hash house. These smoky hideaways emerged in the late 1800s for the benefit of America's urban dwellers. While hash was still a mystery to most Americans, it was becoming known to a growing number of people. First-person accounts of hash experiences were appearing in magazines. Visitors to the 1876 Philadelphia Exposition would have come upon a demonstration of hash smoking at the Turkish display.

Hash houses attracted doctors, artists, writers, and other cultural elites in search of exotic experiences. Located in hotels or upscale private residences, hash houses were the precursor to the more democratic tea pads of the 1940s and 1950s—informal apartment gatherings featuring music,

incense, and reefer smoking. These, in turn, evolved into the hippie pads of the 1960s, with a further breakdown in formality and hygiene.

Our Mr. Kane, who wrote an account of his New York City hash house adventure for *Harper's Monthly* magazine, was first escorted inside a large apartment building. He was immediately assaulted by "a volume of heavily scented air, close upon the heels of which came a deadly sickening odor, wholly unlike anything I had ever smelled."

The unfamiliar air was just the first layer of strangeness for Mr. Kane. Every effort was made to enhance the exotic nature of the experience. Along with other visitors, Kane was handed the required smoking apparel: a silk gown, tasseled smoking

> **Located in hotels or upscale private residences, hash houses were the precursor to the more democratic tea pads of the 1940s and 1950s—informal apartment gatherings featuring music, incense, and reefer smoking.**

LET US TAKE HIGHER   Phone : 13863

EDEN HASHISH CENTRE

Oldest & Favourite Shop In Town Serving You
The Best Nepalese Hash & Ganja
(Available Wholesale & Retail)
COME VISIT US ANY TIME FOR ALL YOUR HASHISH NEEDS

EDEN HASHISH CENTRE
5/1 Basantpur, KATHMANDU
NEPAL
Prop. D. D. Sharma

"Some were smoking, some reclining listlessly upon the pillows, following the tangled thread of a hashish reverie or dream. A middle-aged woman sat bolt upright, gesticulating and laughing quietly to herself; another with lackluster eyes and dropped jaw was swaying her head monotonously from side to side," Kane observed. There was nothing ordinary about Kane's pipe: It was encrusted with multicolored beads and decorated with diamond-shaped patterns and twisted tinsel. He had yet to toke up, but already he'd been dazzled by several sights. The smoke sent him into orbit. The music he heard seemed to ooze from the walls. "I felt extremely happy, at peace with myself and all the world," Kane declared. Hallucinations followed. The end result was an experience both foreign and stimulating for Kane, but one he ultimately turned away from.

cap, and slippers. He took note of the interior design, heavily accented with an Oriental flavor in its carpets and wall hangings. After paying two dollars, Kane was given a small pipe filled with hash and directed toward an area where fellow hash smokers were lounging on cushions and divans.

Kane's account illuminates how, during his life, hash and marijuana use were at the avante garde of American society. It was

200

strongly associated with foreign cultures and traditions. That all changed in the next century as Americans adopted hash and marijuana as their own. Forget about the exotic smoking robe and fancy pillows. In the 1920s, along came the reefer man, dispensing rolled joints on the street for pennies, or maybe a buck or two for the really good stuff.

Recreational marijuana smoking that took root in isolated venues such as tea pads and jazz club back rooms spread to other locations, most notably college dorms of the 1960s, when pot use exploded in America. Thousands of college converts didn't leave marijuana behind after graduation, creating a sizable market for pot consumers—people who regularly bought it and its related paraphernalia. Head shops, a tentative step into legitimate commerce, came into vogue at this time, offering an array of marijuana-smoking supplies, from special pipes and bongs to extra-wide rolling papers and roach clips. Although these incense-saturated markets faded away, a new breed of head shops has emerged today, spiffed up with a boutique look, offering a wide range of smoking accessories and pot-themed clothing and products.

The final economic hurdle—growing your own—was cleared in the 1980s, as American pot farmers took marijuana cultivation to the next level with the development of high-potency sinsemilla. It was like taking a nation weaned on Thunderbird and introducing it to champagne. Market demand was high, ultimately making pot America's number-one cash crop—a remarkable feat for an underground industry. Estimates in the mid-1990s put America's homegrown marijuana market at more than $32 billion, double that of corn and soybeans.

Equally covert is the manner in which people buy, sell, and smoke marijuana, or

Spring
To offer a
marijuana cigarette
marijuana cigarette

even the way they mix it in their brownies. While people readily gather for a social drink, they are more discreet about their bong partners. Still, recreational marijuana use is the most widely practiced taboo. When marijuana smoking was banned by the federal government in 1937, it was estimated that there were no more than fifty thousand Americans who had ever tried it. It wasn't until the late 1960s, a period of great social upheaval, that large numbers of Americans began experimenting with marijuana. By 1969, as many as 12 million Americans had sampled marijuana.

Today, marijuana is entrenched in American society. Look around. Seventy million Americans have tried it. Twelve million Americans are using it on a regular basis. These figures are spread over the entire population, from rural to urban areas, among the educated and noneducated, workers and the unemployed. The largest group of tokers consists of men aged 18 to 25. All this smoking supports an economy and a culture that flourish on a "hush-hush" basis. Despite high-tech and costly efforts to wipe it out, America's marijuana fixation endures, growing more resilient after surviving each effort to stamp it out.

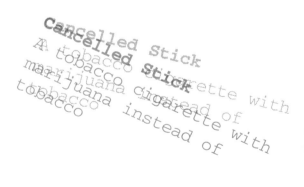

Pot is America's number-one cash crop—a remarkable feat for an underground industry. Estimates in the mid-1990s put America's homegrown marijuana market at more than $32 billion, double that of corn and soybeans.

Cancelled Stick
A tobacco cigarette with marijuana instead of tobacco

The Growing Game

Not long ago, marijuana connoisseurs would have sniffed at the idea of smoking any "home-grown." The quality of American pot was notoriously erratic, and usually poor at best. When Americans began sampling marijuana in large numbers in the late 1960s, they were most likely toking up on pot smuggled from Mexico. A crackdown on this market led to an increase in marijuana from more exotic locales, including Jamaica, Thailand, and Columbia. This higher-potency bud further broadened the gap in quality between foreign blends and weaker homegrown, which was riddled with seeds and twigs and didn't pack an extra kick.

That changed in the late 1970s as federal efforts to cut off foreign supplies spawned a burgeoning homegrown market. It began in remote regions of California, Oregon, and Hawaii and has since spread across the country. Marijuana cultivation is a high-stakes game of cat-and-mouse, pitting sophisticated, adaptive, and proud growers against well-funded and militarily equipped government drug agents.

America's number one cash crop.

Billion-dollar sales weren't on the minds of pot farmers who began in a remote Northern California region known as the Emerald Triangle, a lush landscape covering Humboldt, Trinity, and Mendocino counties. Initial growers were transplanted hippies from urban areas who had flocked to the region

Today, marijuana is entrenched in American society. Look around. Seventy million Americans have tried it. Twelve million Americans are using it on a regular basis.

for its isolation and mild climate—attributes that would later be a valuable asset for clandestine marijuana growers. While at first growing it for themselves, pot farmers quickly discovered a lucrative market for their product. Eventually, federal drug agents moved in during the late 1970s, initiating an annual military-style eradication campaign that continues today.

Bill Ruzzamenti was an agent with the Drug Enforcement Agency during these early marijuana battles. He believes that the paraquat scare more than anything helped jump-start the domestic market. Ruzzamenti says that "hippies and all the folks that were smoking marijuana" were terrified of paraquat. "Being the industrious beavers that they were, they decided to take things into their own hands. The domestic market emerged with a vengeance. They were counterculture dropouts and they started growing marijuana on their own because they didn't trust the Mexican weed," Ruzzamenti points out. "As time went on, people began to see there was a

market for this. As gardens became larger, every Tom, Dick, and Harry who could put a seed in the ground tried to get into the business."

At first, DEA agents found gardens that peaked with one hundred plants. By the mid-1980s, they were discovering ten thousand-plant fields of marijuana. "My grandmother could spot marijuana flying over Humboldt in a 747, there was so much damn marijuana out there. The problem was getting in there and getting the crap out," Ruzzamenti observes.

A similar growing boom took place in Hawaii. The *pakalolo* market, a Hawaiian term for "crazy smoke," was estimated in the 1980s to be at $300 to $400 million, easily more than the state's production of sugar and pineapple combined. Some growers came from the mainland and others were locals. With such potential high payoffs, it didn't take long before the business became cutthroat. Growers had every reason to be paranoid. They had to contend with wild pigs and armed crime gangs, fearing these

> **At first, DEA agents found gardens that peaked with one hundred plants. By the mid-1980s, they were discovering ten thousand-plant fields of marijuana.**

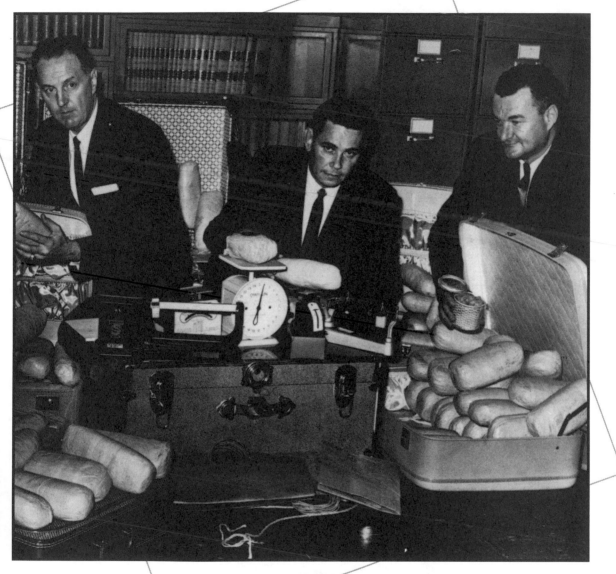

Narcotics agents pose with packages of marijuana in suitcases.

more than local police. Harvest time could be particularly nerve-wracking, as syndicate thugs were known for stealing crops at gunpoint, and sometimes killing growers. One wary farmer told a reporter: "Every year I tell myself I'm through with growing. Then I get paid and the money is unbelievable."

The science of hydroponics enabled growers to forego soil in place of water-soluble nutrients.

Not only was the money mind-blowing, but so was the quality of the pot. The introduction of high-potency sinsemilla was a landmark achievement for America's pot cultivators. Growers took furious pride in their crop. Even Ruzzamenti marvels at how seriously they took their work, noting how growers often went with what was the hottest fertilizer or growing technique, striving each season to put out a better and better product. "They would argue with one another that bat guano produced more leaf than another fertilizer, and all this other crapola," Ruzzamenti remembers.

One year chicken manure was the fertilizer of choice, Ruzzamenti says, and more than 30 metric tons of chicken manure were delivered to the area. "And that's a lot of chicken shit," Ruzzamenti concludes. It was all working. Ruzzamenti recalls seeing tremendous buds in the field—plants so burdened that they would fall over like heavily laden fruit trees.

An initial federal campaign to stop growers was the Sinsemilla Strike Force in 1978, which wiped out more than twelve thousand plants in Humboldt County. Local residents, including politicians and even prosecutors, were lukewarm to the presence of the federal force. A frustrated Humboldt County supervisor remarked, "Why spend money on exotic boy scout raids to eradicate something you can't eradicate." Meanwhile, Mendocino agricultural commissioner Ted Eriksen listed marijuana as the county's leading cash crop in 1979, valued at $90 million. "It's an economic fact of life. We'd be unrealistic to ignore it," he declared.

Richard Davis, a hemp activist, moved to Northern California in the 1970s and began a modest growing effort of no more than 16 plants in a greenhouse. "Thousands of people up there grew—everybody who was up a back road grew. It was obvious," Davis remembers. "We learned how to grow sinsemilla really fast and to lay plants down really fast. We were learning to do all these things and then passing them on to neighbors."

After a few harvests, his small crop was yielding 40 pounds of pot. With prices eventually shooting up to $5,000 per pound, it wasn't hard for even the smallest

Mendocino agricultural commissioner Ted Eriksen listed marijuana as the county's leading cash crop in 1979, valued at $90 million. "It's an economic fact of life. We'd be unrealistic to ignore it," he declared.

growers to strike it rich. But federal eradication efforts took their toll. "They were bringing in helicopters, and then landing and dropping off troops with guns and camo gear. It was like a war zone. It got to be pretty stressful," Davis recalls.

Because federal agents aggressively seize property of suspected growers, many growers prefer planting crops in remote areas of federal park land. That's turned U.S. Forest Service rangers into drug agents, prompting them to roam federal parks with night-stalking equipment searching for marijuana-growing operations. Marijuana growing on federal park land has turned once serene landscapes into violent battlegrounds. Armed "patch pirates," as much as federal agents, threaten growers. They defend their turf on public land with elaborate mechanisms, including booby traps, mines, and guard dogs. Grow areas are sometimes guarded by steel-jaw traps, fish hooks strung along at eye level, and Vietnam-style pits with sharpened sticks. Sometimes hikers and other innocent recreational seekers are snared by these defenses. At one point, park rangers warned the public to avoid 773,000 acres of national forest from Northern California to Eastern Kentucky.

In addition to these military-style defenses, Ruzzamenti remembers one grower who draped red balls on his marijuana crop to make it look like tomato plants from the sky. More sophisticated tactics eventually became the norm. Growers moved indoors to stay in business. This move launched a market for sophisticated indoor growing equipment and the development of the science of hydroponics—growing marijuana in water without soil using water-soluble nutrients.

With growing guidebooks spreading the word, and mail-order companies supplying the equipment, marijuana cultivation spread across the country. Pot cultivation eventually hit the nation's farm belt. Tobacco farmers in Virginia, for example, turned to marijuana after they lost federal price supports in the early 1980s. The reason was money. They could get a whopping $100,000 per acre for a marijuana crop. Officials estimated that there were only about 300 plants found growing in Virginia in 1980, but as many as 43,000 the following year. In the late 1980s, a group of Kentucky growers, dubbed the "Cornbread Mafia," was busted with 182 tons of sinsemilla. A Montana farmer, released after serving 15 months for pot cultivation, told reporters, "The family needed money for food on the table."

Federal agents moved against indoor growers in 1989 with a campaign called "Green Merchant." They raided indoor growing suppliers and retail garden shops in 46 states, confiscating equipment and client lists. The raid sent a chill through the indoor gardening community. Growers responded by maximizing bud production from smaller patches, introducing a tightly spaced growing patch known as the "Sea of Green." Using this compact method, growers can produce potent, full buds in a matter of two months, providing them with several crops a year, as opposed to the single harvest with outdoor growing.

A Montana farmer, released after serving 15 months for pot cultivation, told reporters, "The family needed money for food on the table."

The future may be in cyber-gardens, computer-controlled indoor growing patches with scheduled watering and feeding programs and even a way to signal a grower's pager when security at the patch has been broken. It offers growers a tightly controlled cultivation environment with minimal risk, because they are never present except at planting and harvest.

Pot Games

It's not easy growing an illegal marijuana crop, as experienced cultivator Red Yzandnek will tell you. "You can't just scatter seeds hither and yon in the field and expect to spend your winters partying somewhere in the Caribbean!" Red points out. No, aside from the risks of getting busted, indoor and outdoor growers face a variety of challenges that stand in the way of a successful harvest. Mites may attack your precious crop, and so may deer. Your landlord may discover your indoor grow site and evict you—or turn you in to the cops.

Chapter eight

Before you decide you're up for these risks, you may want to experience the perils of marijuana cultivation and dealing from a much safer perspective—playing a board game. The Cultivation Game is the Monopoly of marijuana growing. It was developed by two British Columbia men who based it on the real experiences of Canadian growers. Red Yzandnek is just one of many composite characters who offer advice and playing instructions for the board game.

The object is to survive at the end of the game with the most plants, having endured narc raids, hungry rabbits, informants, and other devious obstacles. The two designers, Harreson Waymen and John Taylor, say the object of the game is partly educational. "We just want to present the reality of that side of life," Waymen told a reporter. "It allows people to dabble on the dark side without being there." More importantly, though, they urge people to have fun with it.

One initial problem with the game was corrected on the second printing. Stoners who had sat down to play complained that the rules were too hard to follow. Catering to the obviously confused audience, the developers simplified things the second time around.

Once game players have completed a successful harvest with the Cultivation Game, they may want to jump over to Reefer City, the board game about pot dealing. Success in this game requires making the right connections for a deal, avoiding getting busted, and successfully manipulating the market levels for the pot, hash, and mushrooms you sell.

The board is amusing. Players maneuver through sections of Reefer City that include Joint Junction, Marijuana Manor, and Bong Towers. Calculating the money exchanges, moving around the board in the right direction, and plotting strategy can be difficult while high. That's why one of the first instructions is that players should learn the rules while straight.

For less formal entertainment, stoners may simply appropriate various drinking games, substituting bong or pipe hits for required rounds of drinking. Some creative stoners have developed their own bonging games. The rules for one called Zonk are on the Internet. It involves earning bong hits by rolling dice and scoring points. To Zonk means not to score, but it also refers to players who are too stoned to even realize that it's their turn to roll— a common hazard, of course, for any game involving multiple bong hits.

For instance, quality seeds are imported from overseas. Initially, discriminating growers could pick up seed samples at Grateful Dead concerts and other like-minded venues. Now the business has spread to mail-order catalogs and the Internet. Growers have for years been crossbreeding cannabis to extract the best qualities of each seed, creating a line of super buds with complexities of taste, appearance, and quality of high. Indoor growing, with its controlled environment, ensures even greater control over the final product. Potent, healthy buds are now nurtured in attics, garages, alcoves, and even closets.

The Search for a Better Bud

Just getting a marijuana harvest to market is an accomplishment for most growers. But many have loftier goals. Like producers of fine wines, they are obsessed with creating a higher-quality product.

Growers have for years been crossbreeding cannabis to extract the best qualities of each seed, creating a line of super buds with complexities of taste, appearance, and quality of high.

214

High Times magazine, an invaluable resource for marijuana growers, began sponsoring an annual marijuana harvest festival in Holland in 1988. Called the Cannabis Cup, the combination convention and celebration draws marijuana connoisseurs from all over to sample such exotic strains as Haze, Northern Lights, and Skunk, said to be the Dom Perignon of marijuana breeds. Dutch seed companies cheerfully offer samples of their prized seeds, which are sometimes smuggled back to the United States for later planting. If it weren't for the fact that the subject was marijuana, the Cannabis Cup could be mistaken for a legitimate trade show. There are slide presentations, networking sessions, product demonstrations, speeches, and an ultimate award ceremony to crown the best buds in the world.

Large-scale growers initiated impromptu harvest festivals in Northern California and Southern Oregon, where relieved growers proudly showed off their prized buds like beaming farmers displaying blue-ribbon hogs. They traded growing tips, too proud to keep trade secrets to themselves. In this way, the pot being shipped around the country kept getting better and better.

As an offshoot of early harvest gatherings, annual marijuana and hemp festivals held across the country continue to draw hundreds of young followers who camp out in remote areas and celebrate pot culture.

Celebrate Freedom!

The 1998
Freedom
Rally

Music
Speakers & Freedom

Live...Max Creek•The Bentmen•Sam Black Church
Little Wolf & the Mojo featuring Shirley Lewis
Dion Knibbs & The Agitators
Ghost of Tony Gold

October 3rd
High Noon - 5 P.M.
on the Boston Common, Boston, MA

For more info call (781) 944-CANN and check out www.MASSCANN.org

WASH. D.C.
JULY 4
1971 SMOKE
-IN

Let's twist again like we
did last summer!

MAY DAY
IS
JAY DAY

May 1, 1999
THE MILLION MARIJUANA MARCH
London • NYC • S.F. • Chicago • Atlanta • Amsterdam • Glasgow •
Johannesburg • Capetown • Auckland, New Zealand
A Mass Rally and March against
Intolerance Demanding:
Stop All Cannabis Arrests • Stop the Lies •
Release the Medicine • Heal the Sick • End the
Prison State
Cures not Wars

In addition to hosting the Cannabis Cup, *High Times*, founded in 1974, is a one-stop service for growers and pot enthusiasts. Leafing through its glossy pages, stoners can access volumes of valuable information, ranging from the price of an ounce of sinsemilla in various regions of the country to the best places to buy seeds and growing equipment. *Sinsemilla Tips*, which billed itself as the "technical trade journal" of the domestic marijuana industry, came after *High Times* and offered growers everything from simple growing hints to products such as camouflage tarps and nets to avoid overhead detection. The magazine eventually folded, but *High Times* continues to thrive.

As an offshoot of early harvest gatherings, annual marijuana and hemp festivals held across the country continue to draw hundreds of young followers who camp out in remote areas and celebrate pot culture. These festivals—normally held over a long weekend and advertised in magazines such as *High Times*—often feature booths promoting various hemp products and a lineup of pro-marijuana bands and speakers.

Toking Up

Escalating prices have done little to dampen the allure of marijuana. In the 1930s, Americans could buy reefers for as little as a nickel and up to $1 or $2 for high-quality "muggles." Most smokers would congregate in tea pads, rented rooms in hotels that were dimly lit and reeking of incense. Music was as necessary as a light.

By 1967, pot was still relatively cheap, with an ounce selling for as little as $10 to $15. Pot smoking meshed nicely with the emerging hippie culture. Fun-loving

217

dropouts in search of serenity would find a slice of happiness in communal smoking circles, which promoted good will and spiritual contemplation. Marijuana was a visible component of popular "Be-ins" and "Love-ins"— hippie culture staples that introduced many young people to the wonders of the drug. The passing of a joint broke down barriers between strangers and fostered the proper frame of mind to celebrate universal love and understanding.

A survey of Yale seniors in 1969 found that 85 out of 100 had tried pot, and half of them smoked about once a week. Social commentators derided this trend, indicating that the younger generation had lost its long-term vision. "I suspect people who make it a career stop being interested in getting ahead become more passive and tend to live only in the present," Dr. Sidney Cohen, a National Institute of Mental Health director, told reporters.

Let's Make a Deal

Buying marijuana has been relatively easy in America, despite the long prohibition. Pot dealers have never attained the more unsavory reputation of street distributors of harder drugs. Although pot is considered an illegal street drug, pot deals don't happen in the street. Smokers looking to set up a reliable source merely have to ask a few people and a connection is made. A deal is more likely to happen in the comfort of someone's home, not in a back alley.

In the 1930s, people went looking for the reefer man, portrayed in song as an upbeat fellow with some quirky ideas. He sold marijuana already rolled into cigarettes. By the 1960s, bulk sale became the norm. Buyers could score dime bags of Mexican grass with ease during the 1960s. If you had to go outside a safe circle of friends to score some pot in the early 1980s, you could take a less convenient route and drop by a smoke shop. These heavily

Bring Back Cheap Pot

guarded storefronts flourished in urban centers across the country. Sellers shielded by bulletproof glass didn't have to advertise. Store owners kept only a few token items on the shelves to make it look like they were running a legitimate market.

If you wanted home delivery, you could have called Michael Cezar of Greenwich Village. He offered New Yorkers the ultimate in consumer convenience by operating an 800 number for pot deliveries. Just so stoners didn't forget it, he made the number obvious: 1-800-WANT-POT. Cezar, also known as the Pope of Pot, aimed to please. After picking up an order, he rushed a bag of marijuana to a customer's door within an hour. Police, who obviously had little trouble finding Cezar, estimated that he was making $40,000 a day before they shut him down. More discreet marijuana messenger services still operate in New York City.

> **Entering a head shop was intended as a trippy experience. Many featured burning incense, beaded partitions, and a black-light room filled with glowing images.**

Mind Your Head

The emergence of head shops during the 1960s catered to an expanding market for smoking supplies, mostly bongs, rolling papers, and pipes. Until entrepreneurs developed or imported marijuana smoking products, resourceful tokers were often left to their own imagination. The tinfoil pipe was a popular option, as was using any traditional pipe and adapting it for marijuana use. Oriental hash pipes were imported and sold in early head shops, filling the market until American manufacturers began turning out their own brands of pipes and bongs.

Entering a head shop was intended to be a trippy experience. Many featured burning incense, beaded partitions, and a black-light room filled with glowing images. Paraphernalia customers had two aims: to buy artistic, cool-looking supplies for home use, and portable smoking equipment for the road and more discreet public smoking. The market hasn't changed much today. Regular smokers may have a traveling pipe and a reliable bong at home. Stash boxes are optional, but they can be a discarded cigar box or a more ornate boutique item, depending on taste. Because of the pungent odor of sinsemilla, weed lovers know that a tight seal

Greetings from
Bong Canyon

See the incredible sights of Bong Canyon!

is probably the most important function for any stash container. Research indicates that Mason jars and Tupperware serve this purpose well, keeping herb fresh.

Another popular device is a roach clip, a vise-tight grip to hold the burnt end of a joint. The clip allows smokers the opportunity to suck one or two last hits without burning their fingers. If a store-bought clip isn't available, resourceful tokers have been known to make a "crutch" by slitting a match or rolling up a portion of a matchbook cover. Pot heads feel the effort is worth it. The roach contains higher levels of THC than the early part of the joint, since some of it gets trapped there during inhalation.

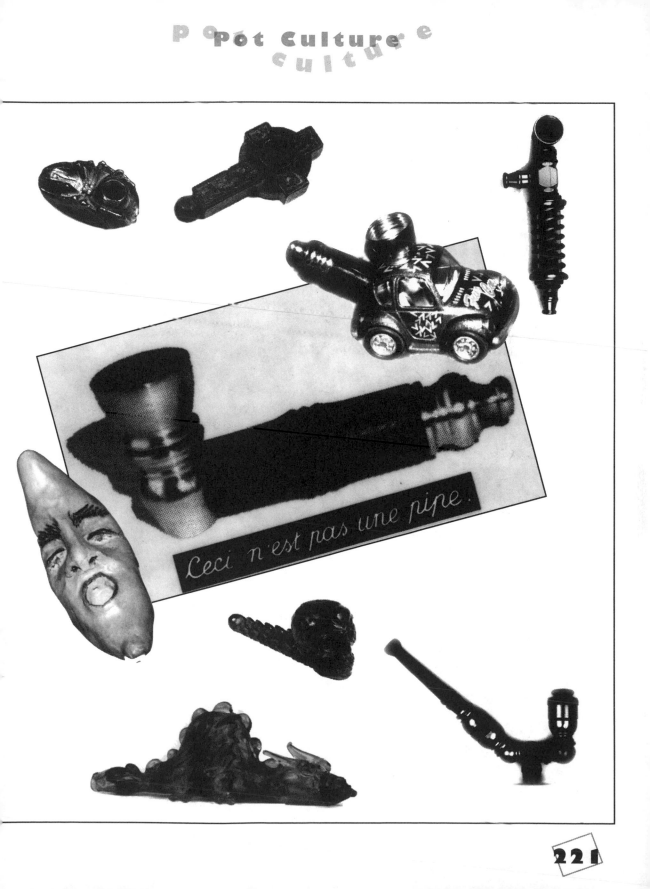

Ceci n'est pas une pipe.

ARE YOU SUPPORTING THE OIL BARONS?

iso-2 is the appliance that lets you make high quality ISO-Hash for about $30 an ounce, also exceptional oils and concentrates comparable to names like Afgani, Lebanese, Columbian and even Thai.

Here's how (actual instructions come with complete details) 1. ISOMERIZATION—The cannabidiol in cannabis is converted to THC. 2. ROTATION—The ISO-2 converts the lower quality Δ8 THC to the more psychedelic Δ8 THC. 3. DECARBOXALATION—The ISO 2 converts the inert THC acids into THC (great for homegrown). 4. PURIFICATION—unwanted unpsychoactive tars are removed making the smoke less harsh. 5. EXTRACTION—The ultra powerful essential oils, hash oil can be removed.

1000 of the original and the price is m

THAI POW

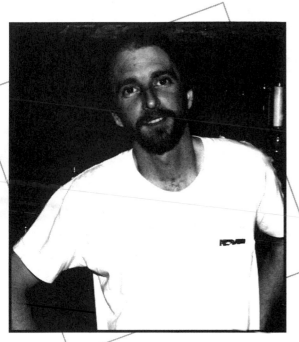

Craig Rubin, proprietor of 2000 B.C.

The New Head Shop

In the 1990s, head shops had a makeover. They were updated and made more upscale by young entrepreneur-activists who believe it's their right to be able to make money from pot-related products. Representative of this trend is Craig Rubin, who owns the 2000 B.C. head shop on Melrose Avenue in Los Angeles, the world-famous tourist destination. He opened in 1993, desiring to make a political statement that Americans should be allowed to smoke pot—and that he should be allowed to profit from it. "I'm a capitalist," Rubin readily admits. "I come from a Republican family. I want to pay my taxes and make a lot of money." And Rubin is not just from any Republican family. When he graduated from Beverly Hills High School, he got a congratulatory greeting from Ronald Reagan.

When police stopped by Rubin's store, they told him he couldn't refer to his water pipes as bongs. Rubin didn't think that was right. So he went out and painted a large window sign that read, "Bongs for Sale." The cops weren't amused. Rubin was arrested, and his case is still pending.

Surely, the Reagans did not know about Rubin's refusal to just say no.

The displays at 2000 B.C. were emptied out by police on October 20, 1994 by the LAPD.

When police stopped by Rubin's store, in October of 1994, they told him he couldn't refer to his water pipes as bongs. Rubin didn't think that was right. So he went out and painted a large window sign that read, "Bongs for Sale." The cops weren't amused. Rubin was arrested, and his case is still pending.

Meanwhile, he has organized hemp rallies at the nearby federal building and hosted pro-marijuana and pro-hemp events at his store. When he goes home at night, Rubin winds down from a busy day by firing up a bowl in his bong. "For me, it's one of the most spiritual things I do in life," he states. "I have a real materialistic life. I work hard and I have a lot of bills. It gives me a few minutes to be thankful."

Rubin says that his mother and grandmother both "bonged." "It's a California thing, to bong it up," he points out. He says his customers come from all over to buy his wide assortment of smoking accessories, from pipes to artistic bongs—er, water pipes— sold on shelves in "Bong Canyon" at the rear of his store. He also sells clothing with pro-hemp slogans and books written by hemp and marijuana activists.

Rubin shows his expertise when making a bong sale to a young secretary. First, he displays bongs ranging from $60 to $600. He then discusses the difference between smoking out of a pipe versus the bong. "When you're home, you're bonging," Craig says, and the young woman nods her head enthusiastically. She settles on a colorful, hand-blown bong for $100 and seems happy with her purchase. "That's pretty. That's cool," she says as he wraps it up. "Marijuana is natural. I don't think of it as a bad thing or illegal at all," she concludes before leaving the store.

Grasshopper
Marijuana user

Pong Bong

The
Worlds
Only
Pipegame

More than just a pipe, the Pong Bong is an exciting game in which two to four tokers battle for the Pong Ball, burning it through winding tunnels of enchanted smoke.

The Bong

The bong has a special place in marijuana culture. Bong technique is a practiced art, with tokers mastering each stage of taking the perfect hit. A correctly inhaled giant bong hit is one way to get completely blasted, or more stoned than with a pipe or joint. Smokers also prefer bongs because of the belief that the water-cooled smoke is less harsh on a toker's lungs. In a quest for even cleaner smoke, a new product called a vaporizer—which looks like a snow globe with a heating element—allegedly extracts harmful vapors from the smoke before a user inhales.

The bong market is especially strong today, with customers willing to spend a few hundred dollars for an artistic pipe for home use. Two brothers who really understand bongs are Adam and Andrew, no last names please, who founded the Skewville Headquarters in New York. They began by altering lunch boxes and turning them into travel kits for bongs. It's a sly trick: The Thermos became the bong. From the outside it looks like an innocent lunch box that might contain a sandwich, milk, and a few cookies.

When they began taking the lunch box bong to parties, they got orders to make more. Eventually, they quit their day jobs and now work full-time making an assortment of bong products. They sell them by mail-order catalog and in stores, and they specialize in bongs that parody mainstream products such as beers and soft drinks. "We worked in advertising and I got fed up with the pressure and the bullshit so I just said, 'Let's just hang out and smoke weed and try and sell our products,'" Adam recalls. "The controversy and the underground nature of it is kind of what keeps us going." They're not sure if they want to hit it that big. "It's our lifestyle first and then trying to figure out how to make a profit out of it," Andrew points out. Spoken like a couple of dedicated bongers.

Jersey Green
Marijuana Gregrown
in New Jersey

A variety of items from Skewville Headquarters.

The Jay

The joint is the workhorse of marijuana consumption. It provides a handy way to transport a dose, and makes sharing convenient. Years ago, reefers were most often rolled up with traditional cigarette papers. By the 1960s, companies such as Job and Zig-Zag were producing rolling papers specifically designed for making joints because they were fatter and longer burning than cigarette papers. The rolling paper market was competitive, and many packages featured eye-catching designs to attract customers and identify the product with a particular style or logo.

In 1971, Robert Stiller noticed that some people were using two papers to twist up a joint. Sensing a business opportunity, he cofounded the E-Z Wider company. The success of the company depended on the niche market of marijuana smokers who rolled their own, but longed for a wider paper. Let's just say that in the world of commerce, such a business premise is a hard sell to investors. Needless to say, it turned into a shrewd business move. The need for a wider paper was great indeed. From an initial $300,000 investment, the company had more than $7 million in sales by 1977. Stiller sold his share of the business in 1980, cashing out without enough money to bankroll the more "legitimate" enterprise of selling gourmet coffee in Vermont.

Other companies have trademarked names such as "Acapulco Gold" and "Panama Red" in the event marijuana cigarettes are one day legal. Until that day, rolling your own remains the only way to make a marijuana cigarette. Some people just can't get the hang of it. They practice and practice, or finally resort to hand-held gadgets that make rolling easier. Rolling, much like the subsequent high, is intensely personal. Some prefer tight, thin joints, while others favor thicker "fatties." Whatever the size, joints are usually twisted at the ends to prevent leakage, leading to the term "twister"— someone who rolls his own joints.

229

The Marijuana Internet

Pot and cyberspace have made a great match. The relative freedom of the Internet has meshed well with the underground nature of marijuana culture and commerce. Tokers who wouldn't feel comfortable walking into a head shop will, seated in their home in front of a computer screen, surf marijuana sites and even order supplies from online outlets. Everyone from serious political and educational groups down to individual marijuana lovers have launched cyber tributes to their beloved weed. So much so that anti-marijuana forces have taken notice. Richard Bonnette, president and CEO of the Partnership For a Drug Free America, observed that, "many of these sites are visually attractive and cyber-hip—rebellious and anti-establishment in theme, persuasive in tone and look and tempting to explore. All of this material is just a click of a computer mouse away, and there's no real way to prevent young people from accessing it."

Just typing in "marijuana" or "hemp" on a search engine yields hundreds of hits, taking a computer user through a virtual tour of marijuana's many facets.

Those interested in political action or scholarly history can visit one of several online drug libraries which offer volumes of information and vital documents about marijuana, including literary references. Dozens of sites are dedicated to medicinal marijuana, allowing supporters to reach out and bond over this issue in cyberspace.

Those with more practical concerns can visit sites offering everything from growing tips to smoking supplies and seeds. Bong-hawking sites include color pictures of a variety of water pipes offered for sale. Ordering seeds is riskier since it's illegal to have them shipped to the United States. But suppliers have clever ways of disguising their products.

Perhaps the most surprising element of marijuana sites on the Internet is how organized they are. The assumption, of course, is that stoners can't follow a logical sequence. But many marijuana sites are linked by networks, making it easy for users to flow from one site to the next, and to travel quickly and efficiently to the places they want to visit.

Rules of the High Way

Although syndicated manners' columnists have yet to write about it, there is a code of etiquette for marijuana smoking. Some people do it crassly, while others inhale with class. Even nonsmokers may find themselves in the middle of a group passing a joint and not know what to do. Faking a massive hit and then passing it along is not really necessary. Even neophytes know the first golden rule: Don't bogart the joint. It's bad form to monopolize the joint in a group setting, an obvious example of bad manners, yet one that is often overlooked. "Bogarting" refers to the dangling cigarette look associated with actor Humphrey Bogart. While Bogie is decidedly cool, there is nothing suave about bogarting.

No double hitting. Take a toke and pass it along. Holding the joint as it burns down through precious bud while you recount a story, or talking in a high tone as you hold the smoke deep in your lungs, are signs of a boorish pot head. Save the stories for after the joint is smoked, when the audience will be more receptive anyway.

In a threesome, with one person standing in the middle, it is tempting but not acceptable to play "centerfield" and take a puff each time you are handed the joint. However, others may not notice this extra dosing if it's attempted in the later rounds. Excessive lip wetting of a passing joint, rendering it limp for the next toker, also lacks consideration. You're sharing a joint, not saliva.

It's wise to determine the potency of the pot before you start smoking. Most experienced smokers know to do this because they always have a determined level of being stoned they want to achieve. A buzz target, so to speak. They

need to know how strong the pot is before deciding how many hits on the joint to take. If the pot is particularly potent, they may take one hit and then wait to measure the effects before taking another. Still others may be in a party mood and perfectly ready to get "wasted." They will toke up with gusto. It is not nice to try and fool the group by understating the potency of the smoke. Even one extra toke can send smokers beyond the limits of their comfortable high.

Because smokers regulate their high according to tolerance and mood, some people may end up passing on the second round. However, this doesn't mean that they are out of the action. Therefore, it would be rude not to offer the joint to a person who had previously passed.

Keep track of the passing order. As the joint goes around, someone will pass it to you, and after you're finished, you will pass it along to someone else. After a round or two, many people simply forget where they are in the passing order. You'll see them fumbling with the lit joint, not really sure in which direction to pass. If the pot is particularly strong, a

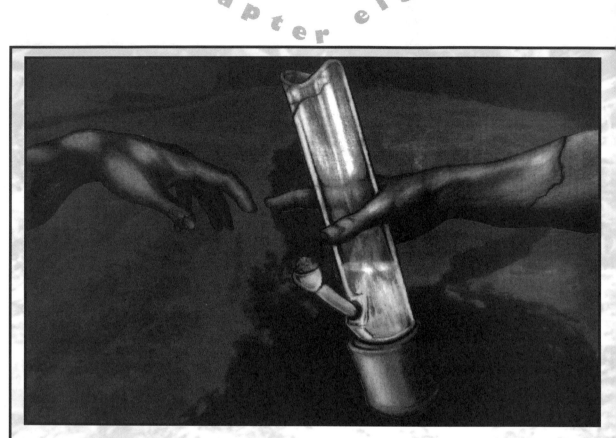

And God said, "Go forth and bongeth...just don't spilleth."

smoker may end up holding the joint and not even knowing it. The roach may be smoked right then. But if everyone is sated, it is customary to offer it to the person who brought along the joint. A generous person will simply offer the roach to someone with the thoughtful words of "save it for later." With the potency of today's pot, the one or two hits left in even the smallest of roaches can be enough for a significant high.

And one bong rule: under no circumstance is it OK to spill bong water.

Associations and Organizations

Education, Legalization, and Research

Agricultural Hemp Association
Nonprofit 501 (c)(3) hemp advocacy group
P.O. Box 8671
Denver, CO 80201
Tel: (303) 298-9414
www.earthlink.net/ahahemp

Alterna's Applied Research Laboratories
10877 Wilshire Blvd., 12th Floor
Los Angeles, CA 90024
Tel: (888) 4-ALTERNA
Fax: (310) 824-0082
www.4alterna.com

BACH (Business Alliance for Commerce in Hemp)
P.O. Box 1716
El Cerrito, CA 94530-2427
Tel: (510) 215-8326
www.chrisconrad.com

Cannabis Reform Coalition on the University of Mass. Amherst Campus
verdant@twain.ucs.umass.edu

CHA (Coalition for Hemp Awareness)
P.O. Box 9266
Chandler Heights, AZ 85227
Tel: (602) 988-9355

Consolidated Growers and Processors Inc.
P.O. Box 2228
Monterey, CA 93942-2228
Tel: (888) 333-8CGP
www.congrowpro.com

David Borden of the Drug Reform Coordination Network
borden@eff.org

Electronic Frontier Foundation
barlow@eff.org
Hemp Industries Association (HIA)
P.O. Box 1080
Occidental, CA 95465
Tel: (707) 874-3648
www.thehia.org

Hemp Program of Health, Canada
122 Bank Street, 3rd Floor
Ottawa, Ontario K1A 1B9
Tel: (613) 954-6524

Institute for Hemp, educational and political center
instforhemp@delphi.com

Jack Herer
Help End Marijuana Prohibition
5632 Van Nuys Blvd., #310
Van Nuys, CA 91401

Kentucky Hemp Growers Cooperative Association, Inc.
P.O. Box 8395
Lexington, KY 40533
Tel: (606) 252-8954

The Merry Hempsters
P.O. Box 1301
Eugene, OR 97440
Tel: (541) 345-9317
www.pacinfo.com/merryhemp

NORML Foundation
1001 Connecticut Ave., N.W.
Suite 710
Washington, DC 20036
Tel: (202) 483-8751
Fax: (202) 483-0057
E-mail: foundation@norml.org
www.norml.org

Partnership for a Drug-Free America
405 Lexington Ave.
New York, NY 10174
(800) 729-6686
www.drugfreeamerica.org

President Clinton's office
president@whitehouse.gov

True North Hemp Company LTD
#10760, 10324-WHYTE (82) Ave.
Edmonton, Alberta T6E-1Z8
Canada
Tel/Fax: (403) 437-4367

Vermont Hemporium Office
vthemp@aol.com

Medicinal Marijuana

Los Angeles Cannabis Resource Center
7494 Santa Monica Blvd., #215
West Hollywood, CA 90046

The University of Mississippi
University, MS 38677

Miscellaneous Organizations and Contacts

Astounding Graphics
620 S. Raymond Ave., Suite 4
Pasadena, CA 91105
(626) 683-2602
www.astoundingcards.com

Bernie Brightman
Stash Records
P.O. Box 1337
New York, NY 10276

Charles Alvison
Testclean.com
2911 N.W. 122 St., Suite 149
Oklahoma City, OK 73120
www.testclean.com

Cris Moeller
30620 N. 63 St.
Cave Creek, AZ 85331

The Museum of Questionable
Medical Devices
201 Main St., S.E.
Minneapolis, MN 55416
or
Ofc. address
549 Turnpike Road
Golden Valley, MN 55416

Rick Loomis
P.O. Box 1467
Scottsdale, AZ 85252

Bookstores and Publications

Commercial Hemp
Suite 302-305 Hamilton Street
Vancouver, B.C. V6B 2R1
Canada
Tel: (888) 718-5577
www.wisenoble.com

The Great Book of Hemp
by Rowan Robinson
Park Street Press,
an imprint of Inner Traditions Int.,
Ltd.
Rochester, VT 05767
Copyright © 1996 by Park Street Press

Hemp BC
307 W. Hastings
Vancouver, B.C. V6B 1H6
Canada
Tel: (604) 681-4620

Hemp Horizons
by John W. Roulac
Chelsea Green Publishing
P.O. Box 428
White River Junction, VT 05001

Hemp Today: The Environmental
Newspaper
Formerly known as Hemp Magazine
1533 Westheimer
Houston, TX 77006
Tel: (713) 523-3199

Hemptech Inc.
P.O. Box 1716
Sebastopol, CA 95473
Tel: (707) 823-2800
www.hemptech.com

HempWorld/Hemp Pages
P.O. Box 550
Forestville, CA 95436
Tel: (707) 887-7508
www.hempworld.com

High Times
235 Park Ave. S., 5th Floor
New York, NY 10003
Tel: (212) 260-0200

Marc Emery, publisher of Marijuana
and Hemp Newsletter in Canada
marc_emery@mindlink.bc.ca

Mari Kane, publisher of Hemp World
Magazine
hemplady@crl.com

Quick American Archives
1635 East 22nd Street
Oakland, CA 94606
Tel: (510) 535-0495

Retail

Distributors

Azida, Inc.
P.O. Box 247
Elfrida, AZ 85610
Tel: (800) 603-6601
E-mail:
highdeserthemp@theriver.com

Ecolution
2812 E-Merrilee Drive
Fairfax, VA 22031
Tel: (888) ECO-HEMP
www.ecolution.com

Ohio Hempery
P.O. Box 18
Guysville, OH 45735
Tel: (800) BUY-HEMP
www.hempery.com

Planet Hemp
423 Broome Street
New York, NY 10013-3226
(800) 681-HEMP

Real Goods Trading Corp.
555 Leslie Street
Ukiah, CA 95482
Tel: (800) 762-7325
www.realgoods.com

Schermerhorn
12922 Florence Avenue
Santa Fe Springs, CA 90670
Tel: (800) 932-9395

Hemp

2000 B.C.
The Hemp Store
8260 Melrose Ave.
Los Angeles, CA 90046
(323) 782-0760
www.2000BC.COM

All Points East
P.O. Box 221776
Carmel, CA 93922
Tel: (831) 655-4367

Deep E Company
404 N.W. 10th Ave., Ste. 201
Portland, OR 97209
Tel: (888) 233-3373
www.deepeco.com

Exotic Gifts, a hemp importer and
distributor
exotic@northcoast.com

Frederick Brewing Co.
4607 Wedgewood Blvd.
Frederick, MD 21703
Tel: (301) 694-7899
www.fredbrew.com

Fremont Hemp Company
3526-C Fremont Place N.
Seattle, WA 98103
Tel: (206) 632-HEMP
www.fremonthemp.com

Friendly Stranger
226 Queen Street W.
Toronto, Ontario M5V 1Z6
Canada
Tel: (416) 591-1570
www.friendlystranger.com

Harvest House
2816 W. North Ave.
Chicago, IL 60647
Tel: (773) 292-1395
Fax: (773) 292-9471

Hemp BC, retail, online virtual store
www.hempbc.com

The Hemp Club, Inc.
3418 A Park Avenue
Montreal, QC H2X 2H5
Canada
Tel: (514) 845-4993
thehempclubthc@hotmail.com

Hemp Shak
844 Monterey
San Luis Obispo, CA 93401
Tel: (805) 543-0760

Hemp Traders
2132 Colby Avenue #5
Los Angeles, CA 90025
Tel: (310) 914-9557
hemptrader@aol.com

Hemp Wine America
(888) 520-9463
www.hempwine.com

Hempfields Natural Goods
P.O. Box 5294
Hilo, HI 96720
Tel: (888) HEMP-JAVA
www.hempfields.com

Hempstead Company
2060 Placentia, #B-2
Costa Mesa, CA 92627
Tel: (800) 284-HEMP
www.hempstead.com

Hempzels
A Division of No Problem, Inc.
P.O. Box 13
New Holland, PA 17557
800-USE-HEMP

Island Hemp Wear
P.O. Box 690
Kekaha, HI 96752
Tel: (808) 337-1487
www.hawaiian.net/hemp

Living Tree Paper
1430 Wilamette St., Ste. 367
Eugene, OR 97401
Tel: (800) 309-2974
www.livingtreepaper.com

Pickering International
888 Post Street
San Francisco, CA 94109
Tel: (415) 474-2288
www.pickhemp.com

Rio Rockers
Tel: (831) 426-0265
Fax: (831) 469-3011
E-mail: al@rioproducts.net
www.rioproducts.net

Santa Barbara Hemp Company
15 W. Anapamu Street
Santa Barbara, CA 93101
Tel: (805) 965-7170
www.santabarbarahempco.com

Tribal Fiber, Inc.
P.O. Box 19755
Boulder, CO 80308
Tel: (303) 415-0478

Paraphernalia

Reefer City Productions
307 W. 7th St., #275
Fort Worth, TX 7602

Roll-Your-Own
Pure Hemp Rolling Paper
43 Melville Ave.
Toronto, Ont.
Canada
M6G 1Y1
Tel: (416) 535-3497
Fax: (416) 535-1616

Rub & Dub
C.P. 2086 - E. Levante
40100 Bologna
Italy

Skewville Headquarters
2609 28 St.
Skewville, NY 11102
www.skewville.com

Slice of Life Games
P.O. Box 41011
Victoria BC
V8Y 3C8
Canada

THC
P.O. Box 16996
Beverly Hills, CA 90209
Tel: (310) 273-9633
Fax: (310) 278-5151
www.thc.com

While every effort has been made to contact manufacturers, companies, and individuals, some sources of certain photographs and illustrations were impossible to track down. Any uncredited image brought to our attention by its owner will be credited in future editions.

Slice of Life Games: 8 (top), 211 (all)

Bill Bridges Photography: 8 (bottom), 14, 82, 90, 98 (all), 99, 105, 107, 132 (top), 135, 136, 139 (upper left), 142, 144, 146 (all), 150, 203, 206, 224

The Great Book of Hemp by Rowan Robinson: 9, 10, 11, 12, 86, 147

Astounding Graphics: 15, 17, 28, 29 (all), 164, 165, 171, 173 (upper left), 182, 183

The Nostalgia Collection: 16, 32, 33, 34, 35, 36, 39, 42, 54, 62, 70 (all), 81, 100 (upper left), 113, 134 (bottom right), 140, 141 (bottom), 158, 160, 166, 200 (upper left), 205, 207, 209, 215, 216 (upper and lower right), 218 (bottom), 221 (all), 222 (all), 226 (all), 233, 234

Hollywood Photo Archives: 50, 161, 162, 172, 173 (upper and lower right), 174 (all), 175, 176 (all), 184, 186, 187, 188 (all), 190, 191, 192, 193, 195, 209

Jorge Pacheco Cartoons & Illustrations: 18, 55, 77, 79, 80, 83, 120, 124, 128, 196

Harvest House: 19, 152, 153

Planet Hemp: 20, 133 (all)

C.K.: 21, 47 (lower right), 48, 87 (all), 169, 200 (bottom), 214, 218 (top), 225 (all),

Bernie Brightman: 23, 119, 178 (all), 179

Cris Moeller: 24 (upper left), 72

The Museum of Questionable Medical Devices: 30 (all), 38

NORML Foundation: 41, 45, 47 (upper left), 56, 58, 59 (all), 61, 66, 88 (lower right), 91 (top), 94, 134 (bottom left), 177, 216 (upper left)

Partnership for a Drug-Free America: 44

Collection of Rick Loomis: 52

Saul Rubin: 53, 57, 126 (all), 138, 155, 223 (upper left)

Testclean.com: 65, 68, 69, 71

THC: 88 (upper left), 208

Los Angeles Cannabis Resource Center Archive: 91 (bottom), 92 (all), 93

The University of Mississippi: 100 (lower right), 101, 102 (all), 103 (all)

Hemp Wine America: 132 (bottom)

Alterna's Applied Research Laboratory: 137

Rio Rockers: 139 (upper right)

Ohio Hempery: 141 (top)

Hemp for Victory: 145 (all), 149, 154

From the Collections of the Henry Ford Museum and Greenfield Village: 151

Frederick Brewing Company: 156

Roll-Your-Own Pure Hemp Rolling Paper: 157 (top)

Hempzels, a Division of No Problem, Inc.: 157 (bottom)

Chongo Productions: 181, 189

Reefer City Productions: 212 (all)

2000 B.C.: 220, 223 (lower right)

Skewville Smokables: 228 (all)

Collection of Loris Piccinato: 230 (all)

Books Available From Santa Monica Press

The Book of Good Habits
by Dirk Mathison
$9.95

Collecting Sins
by Steven Sobel
$13

Health Care Handbook
by Mark Cromer
$12.95

Helpful Household Hints
by June King
$12.95

How to Find Your Family Roots
by William Latham
$12.95

**How to Win Lotteries,
Sweepstakes, and Contests**
by Steve Ledoux
$12.95

Letter Writing Made Easy!
by Margaret McCarthy
$12.95

Letter Writing Made Easy! Volume 2
by Margaret McCarthy
$12.95

Offbeat Golf
A Swingin' Guide to a Worldwide Obsession
by Bob Loeffelbein
$17.95

Offbeat Marijuana
The Life & Times of the
World's Grooviest Plant
by Saul Rubin
$19.95

Offbeat Museums
The Collections and Curators of America's
Most Unusual Museums
by Saul Rubin
$19.95

**Past Imperfect:
How Tracing Your Family Medical History
Can Save Your Life**
by Carol Daus
$12.95

What's Buggin' You?
by Michael Bohdan
$12.95

Order Form

SANTA MONICA PRESS

Toll Free 1.800.784.9553

	Quantity	Amount
The Book of Good Habits ($9.95)	_____	_____
Collecting Sins ($13)	_____	_____
Health Care Handbook ($12.95)	_____	_____
Helpful Household Hints ($12.95)	_____	_____
How to Find Your Family Roots ($12.95)	_____	_____
How to Win Lotteries,... ($12.95)	_____	_____
Letter Writing Made Easy! ($12.95)	_____	_____
Letter Writing Made Easy! Volume 2 ($12.95)	_____	_____
Offbeat Golf ($17.95)	_____	_____
Offbeat Marijuana ($19.95)	_____	_____
Offbeat Museums ($19.95)	_____	_____
Past Imperfect...($12.95)	_____	_____
What's Buggin' You? ($12.95)	_____	_____

Shipping & Handling

1 book	$3.00
Each additional book	$0.50

Subtotal _____

Shipping and Handling (see left) _____

CA residents add 8.25% sales tax _____

TOTAL _____

Name _____

Address _____

City/State/Zip _____

Card Number _____ Exp. _____

Signature _____ □ Visa   □ Mastercard

☐ Enclosed is my check or money order payable to:

Santa Monica Press • P.O. Box 1076 • Dept. 1051 • Santa Monica, CA 90406-1076
Tel. 310.395.4658 • Fax 310.395.6394 • www.santamonicapress.com